TRADITIONAL
AFRICAN
RECIPES

TRADITIONAL
AFRICAN
RECIPES

AUTHENTIC CLASSIC DISHES FROM ALL OVER AFRICA
ADAPTED FOR THE WESTERN KITCHEN – ALL SHOWN
STEP BY STEP IN 300 SIMPLE-TO-FOLLOW PHOTOGRAPHS

ROSAMUND GRANT

southwater

To Patricia Elonge, Nii Noi, Efua, Princess Ajibe Ebanja and Hazel Ayesha Daniels

This edition is published by Southwater, an imprint of Anness Publishing Ltd,
by Road, Wigston, Leicestershire LE18 4SE; info@anness.com

www.southwaterbooks.com; www.annesspublishing.com

the images in this book and would like to investigate using them for
ublishing, promotions or advertising, please visit our website
www.practicalpictures.com for more information.

Publisher Joanna Lorenz
Managing Editor Linda Fraser
Food Editor Anne Hildyard
Copy Editor Christine Ingram
Designer Siân Keogh
Photography and Styling Patrick McLeavey, assisted by Jo Brewer
Food for Photography Annie Nichols, assisted by Curtis Edwards
Illustrator Madeleine David
Pictures on page 1 and page 7 Zefa Pictures Ltd

© Anness Publishing Ltd 2012

A CIP catalogue record for this book is available from the British Library.

NOTES

For all recipes, quantities are given in both metric and imperial measures and,
where appropriate, in standard cups and spoons. Follow one set of measures,
but not a mixture, because they are not interchangeable.
Standard spoon and cup measures are level.
1 tsp = 5ml, 1 tbsp = 15ml, 1 cup = 250ml/8fl oz.
Australian standard tablespoons are 20ml. Australian readers should use
3 tsp in place of 1 tbsp for measuring small quantities.
American pints are 16fl oz/2 cups. American readers should use
20fl oz/2.5 cups in place of 1 pint when measuring liquids.
Electric oven temperatures in this book are for conventional ovens. When using a fan oven,
the temperature will probably need to be reduced by about 10–20°C/20–40°F.
Since ovens vary, you should check with your manufacturer's instruction book for guidance.
Medium (US large) eggs are used unless otherwise stated.

PUBLISHER'S NOTE

Although the advice and information in this book are believed to be accurate and true at the time
of going to press, neither the authors nor the publisher can accept any legal responsibility or
liability for any errors or omissions that may have been made nor for any inaccuracies nor for
any loss, harm or injury that comes about from following instructions or advice in this book.

The author would like to thank all those people who kindly gave their time –
and their recipes: Bethlehem, Ethiopian restaurateur and owner of Senke in North London,
who taught her many traditional dishes from their menu.
Neema Nsubuga, from Bukoba on Lake Victoria in Tanzania, who helped her with ingredients.
Her cousin, Nene Elonge, a talented and versatile cook, who made exquisite
Cameroonian dishes and gave lots of creative ideas with plantains.
She would like to thank Millicent for her Kenyan recipes,
Donu for her lovely Lobster Piri Piri and advice on Nigerian cooking.
Lastly, Doris and Curtis for helping to test the recipes – and for painstakingly
counting every ounce to achieve accuracy.

CONTENTS

Introduction *6*

Soups and Appetizers *10*

Meat and Poultry *26*

Fish and Seafood *46*

Vegetable and Vegetarian Dishes *58*

Side Dishes *68*

Desserts *88*

Index *96*

INTRODUCTION

Entertaining with food and music is integral to African social life and family, friends and festivity are closely associated in both rural and urban homes. "No advance warning required" is an attitude that prevails and, in fact, cooking only for the members of your household can get you a bad reputation! So, many hosts and hostesses make it their business to ensure that there are always extra titbits around for unexpected visitors who might call by at any time of the day or evening.

Foreigners are often amazed by the warmth that is lavished upon them when they only expected a cup of tea!

Rigid recipes are rare, most African cooks inherit vague techniques by word of mouth and then go on to develop their skills by experimenting with different ingredients and cooking methods. They often create new and interesting combinations by following their instincts rather than written instructions. So it isn't too fanciful to talk about cooking that comes from the heart.

Morocco

Sierra Leone

Ghana

Nigeria

Cameroon

Ethiopia

Kenya

Tanzania

Mozambique

In some regions meat and fish are often scarce and only eaten on festive occasions. But the economic restraints they endure do not prevent Africa's many gourmets from creating delectable dishes. Throughout Africa, vegetable, bean and lentil dishes are extremely popular and meat is often used merely as one of a number of flavourings, rather than as a main ingredient. In West Africa, spicy tomato-based sauces are very well-liked, while in the east of the continent, the influence of Indian cooking on the traditional African cuisine makes for an interesting and delicious culinary adventure.

In this book, along with dozens of colourful and tasty, traditional recipes, such as Joloff Chicken and Rice, there are plenty of variations and adaptations of authentic dishes, such as Kachumbali Salad, as well as several contemporary

dishes, such as Bean and Gari Loaf, and Fish with Red Onions, Lemon and Coriander, created using traditional ingredients, herbs and spices.

Eating in Africa is a unique and exciting experience, throughout the continent cooks use the same or similar ingredients, but often prepare and cook them in different ways according to local tradition and custom. For example, in some West African countries okra is chopped very finely, until it is reduced almost to a pulp, giving a rich silky consistency to sauces and soups, while elsewhere the okra is often left whole to give a completely different result.

The essential staples – yams, cassava, green bananas and plantains – are used throughout Africa, either on their own or combined with others to make Fu Fu, a popular accompaniment to all sorts of savoury dishes.

Sweet potatoes, coconuts, okra, a huge variety of green vegetables, beans and pulses, nuts, and grains, such as corn, are all common cooking ingredients, while all sorts of wonderful, tropical fruits, such as mangoes, avocados and paw paw, are a familiar sight and are eaten at any time of the day – not just reserved for dessert.

Two ingredients are worth a particular mention. Chillies add spice and flavour to many dishes, but even adventurous cooks would do well to slowly accustom themselves to the zingingly hot dishes in

Fresh ripe pineapples are in plentiful supply in this bustling fruit market.

Collecting – and cracking – fresh coconuts is very often a family affair.

which Africans specialize and revel! Less well-known is palm oil, which is unlike any other oil and should be used sparingly – its distinctive, strong flavour is definitely an acquired taste.

This book is largely due to the generosity and enthusiasm of many wonderful women who have welcomed me into their homes to share their culinary skills and treasured secrets. Many of these women had learned recipes from their mothers and grandmothers, others had just acquired a taste and flair for African cooking from visits to the continent. I have travelled to north and west Africa and over the years have also been lucky enough to watch and share with my relatives and friends some of their many glorious meals.

Although you may be unfamiliar

with some of the ingredients mentioned in my recipes, you will find that most are available in large supermarkets, street markets, and in particular, African and Asian stores, which often stock a huge variety of fresh fruit and vegetables. If you are not sure about an ingredient, quiz the shop keeper, or even shoppers themselves – I always find that the best way to understand and become familiar with new ingredients is to ask about them.

African cooking is all about being creative and having a feel for the food. My suggestion is to try the recipes, adapt them if you like, and create your own taste of Africa.

INGREDIENTS

ALLSPICE
Available whole or ground, allspice are small, dark brown berries similar in size to large peppercorns. They can be used in sweet or savoury dishes and have a flavour of nutmeg, cinnamon and clove, hence the name.

AUBERGINE
In Africa, a yellowish white variety of aubergine is grown, known as a garden egg. These are not widely available in this country but the common purple/black aubergine can be used instead.

BLACK-EYED BEANS
This pulse originally came from Africa, where it is a staple food. It can be soaked overnight or boiled without soaking if you allow an extra 1/2 hour. It is used in all sorts of African dishes, soups, stews, rice dishes, salads and snacks. Available in most large supermarkets, delicatessens and health food stores.

Clockwise from top left: Yam, okra, christophene, sweet potatoes.

CORIANDER
Also known as cilantro or Chinese parsley, the leaves of this herb look like parsley and add an intense pungent flavour to stews and soups.

CASSAVA
This tropical vegetable has tuberous roots with a brown skin and hard starchy white flesh. Dried and ground, it makes cassava flour and gari (see right).

Clockwise from top left: Groundnut oil, palm oil, cashew nuts.

CHILLIES
A wide variety of chillies or hot peppers are grown in West Africa. One of the hottest is the fat and fiery Scotch Bonnet. It has a spicy smell and flavour and can be red, green, yellow or brown. Always take care when handling any hot chilli as the oils can be very painful if they touch the eyes or any sensitive area. If you don't want very fiery food, remove the seeds and core of chillies, thinly slice and add sparingly to a stew or broth until you know the "heat" you require.

CHRISTOPHENE
This is a pear-shaped vegetable with a cream-coloured or green skin. It has a bland flavour, similar to squash or marrow.

COCONUT
The flesh and milk of the coconut is used widely in Africa. Coconut milk is available in cans from African and Asian grocers, but make sure to buy the unsweetened variety. Creamed coconut is widely available and can be used grated onto casseroles or used to make coconut milk by dissolving it in boiling water.

DRIED SHRIMPS
These small shrimps, available with or without shells, are dried in the sun. They are a popular seasoning in African cuisine and add a distinctive flavour to stews and broths. Available from African, Caribbean and Asian food stores.

EGUSI
This is made from either melon seeds or the seeds of a fruit that is a cross between a gourd and a pumpkin. The seeds are like small almonds and are often ground for recipes. It is available from most African food shops.

FIVE-SPICE POWDER
This reddish-brown powder is a combination of five ground spices – star anise seed, fennel, clove, cinnamon and Szechwan pepper. Use sparingly, it has a wonderful flavour and aroma but can be dominant.

Clockwise from top left: Pomfret, red snapper, tilapia, dried shrimp.

GARI
This is a coarse-ground flour made from cassava and is used in a number of African recipes. It is available from African, Caribbean and Asian food shops.

Mangoes – small and large.

Aubergine – large and small and garden egg types.

GREEN BANANAS

These are unripe bananas, although only certain varieties are used as a green vegetable. They are usually boiled, with or without their skins. A little oil added when boiling helps to keep the saucepan clean. (To peel green bananas, see plantains.)

GROUNDNUT PASTE

Used in West African cooking mainly to make delicious sauces, pure groundnut paste is difficult to find, so substitute natural smooth or crunchy peanut butter. Shelled and skinned roasted peanuts can be ground either with a mortar and pestle or in a spice or coffee grinder.

MANGO

These beautiful fruits, shaped like enormous pips, can be as large as melons or as small as apples. They have a vivid golden flesh with a deep flavour. Green mangoes are used for chutneys and to add tartness to casseroles and stews.

MUNG BEANS

Sometimes known as green gram or golden gram. They are small, bright green dried beans, available from large supermarkets or from Asian or African food stores.

OILS

Palm oil A bright orange/red oil extracted from the fruits of the oil palm. There is really no substitute for palm oil – it gives food a very authentic flavour, although use sparingly, as it can be rather overpowering. Available in most Asian, African or Caribbean food shops.

Groundnut oil Made from peanuts, this is another essential cooking oil if you want to achieve an authentic African flavour. Available from most Asian and African food shops and from large supermarkets.

OKRA

Also known as ladies fingers, these are extremely popular in African cookery and were one of the vegetables taken by the slaves to the Caribbean where they are also widely used. When buying okra, avoid the larger varieties and choose small, firm ones. Wash and dry them *before* topping, tailing and cutting up, this will prevent them from getting too sticky.

PLANTAINS

These members of the banana family can be green, yellow or almost black according to their ripeness. They are inedible raw, but once cooked, either boiled, fried, baked or roasted, have a wonderful flavour. To peel a plantain, remove the top and tail with a sharp knife and cut in half. Make three or four slits lengthways in the skin without cutting the flesh. Lift off the edge of a slit and run the tip of your thumb under the edge, lengthways, peeling back and removing all of the skin.

Green bananas and plantains.

Clockwise from top: Gari, black cardamom pods, egusi, ground egusi, mung beans, black-eyed beans (centre).

RED KIDNEY BEANS

All sorts of beans and pulses are used in African cookery for casseroles, soups and stews. Red kidney beans are poisonous when raw and should be soaked for several hours or overnight and then boiled rapidly for 10–15 minutes before simmering until tender or cooked according to the recipe.

SWEET POTATO

The skin of the sweet potato ranges in colour from white to pink to reddish brown. There are several varieties, but the white-fleshed, red-skinned variety is most commonly used in African cookery. Sweet potatoes can be boiled, roasted, fried, creamed or baked in their skins – and are ideal for both sweet and savoury dishes.

YAM

These come in all sizes – some varieties are huge – so when buying, ask for a piece the size you need. The flesh is either yellow or white and can be eaten boiled, roasted, baked, mashed or made into chips.

SOUPS
AND
APPETIZERS

In some African countries, soup is the whole meal, made using meat or fish, and dried beans or vegetables and served with a staple food such as fufu, ground rice or boiled yam. One of the most popular soups is Groundnut Soup, made from peanuts, and many African soups are thickened with beans or pulses, while in others the vegetables are chopped so they break up and thicken the broth. Many of the soups in this section have been created using African ingedients are in the style of soups I came across in my travels. The appetizers can be served as snacks or for light lunches, picnics and parties. They are quick, easy and taste good too.

Lamb, Bean and Pumpkin Soup

INGREDIENTS

Serves 4

115g/4oz split black-eyed beans,
  soaked for 1–2 hours, or overnight
675g/1½ lb neck of lamb, cut into
  medium-size chunks
5ml/1 tsp chopped fresh thyme, or
  2.5ml/½ tsp dried
2 bay leaves
1.2 litres/2 pints/5 cups stock or water
1 onion, sliced
225g/8oz pumpkin, diced
2 black cardamom pods
7.5ml/1½ tsp ground turmeric
15ml/1 tbsp chopped fresh coriander
2.5ml/½ tsp caraway seeds
1 fresh green chilli, seeded and chopped
2 green bananas
1 carrot
salt and freshly ground black pepper

1 Drain the black-eyed beans, place
them in a saucepan and cover with
fresh cold water.

2 Bring the beans to the boil, boil
rapidly for 10 minutes and then
reduce the heat and simmer, covered
for 40–50 minutes until tender, adding
more water if necessary. Remove from
the heat and set aside to cool.

3 Meanwhile, put the lamb in a large
saucepan, add the thyme, bay leaves
and stock or water and bring to the
boil. Cover and simmer over a
moderate heat for 1 hour, until tender.

4 Add the onion, pumpkin,
cardamoms, turmeric, coriander,
caraway, chilli and seasoning and stir.
Bring back to a simmer and then cook,
uncovered, for 15 minutes until the
pumpkin is tender, stirring occasionally.

5 When the beans are cool, spoon into
a blender or food processor with
their liquid and blend to a smooth purée.

6 Cut the bananas into medium slices
and the carrot into thin slices. Stir
into the soup with the beans and cook
for 10–12 minutes, until the vegetables
are tender. Adjust seasoning and serve.

Fish and Okra Soup

The inspiration for this soup came from a Ghanaian recipe – chop the okra for a more authentic consistency.

INGREDIENTS

Serves 4
2 green bananas
50g/2oz/4 tbsp butter or margarine
1 onion, finely chopped
2 tomatoes, peeled and finely chopped
115g/4oz okra, trimmed
225g/8oz smoked haddock or cod
    fillet, cut into bite-size pieces
900ml/1½ pints/3¾ cups fish stock
1 fresh chilli, seeded and chopped
salt and freshly ground black pepper
chopped fresh parsley, to garnish

1 Slit the skins of the green bananas and place in a large saucepan. Cover with water, bring to the boil and cook over a moderate heat for about 25 minutes or until the bananas are tender. Transfer to a plate and leave to cool.

2 Melt the butter or margarine in a large saucepan and sauté the onion for about 5 minutes until soft. Stir in the chopped tomatoes and okra and fry gently for a further 10 minutes.

3 Add the fish, fish stock, chilli and seasoning. Bring to the boil, then reduce the heat and simmer for about 20 minutes or until the fish is cooked through and flakes easily.

4 Peel the cooked bananas and cut into slices. Stir into the soup, heat through for a few minutes and then ladle into soup bowls. Sprinkle with parsley and serve.

Plantain and Corn Soup

INGREDIENTS

Serves 4

25g/1oz/2 tbsp butter or margarine
1 onion, finely chopped
1 garlic clove, crushed
275g/10oz yellow plantains, peeled
    and sliced
1 large tomato, peeled and chopped
175g/6oz/1 cup sweetcorn
5ml/1 tsp dried tarragon, crushed
900ml/1½ pints/3¾ cups vegetable or
    chicken stock
1 green chilli, seeded and chopped
pinch of grated nutmeg
salt and freshly ground black pepper

1 Melt the butter or margarine in a saucepan over a moderate heat, add the onion and garlic and fry for a few minutes until the onion is soft.

2 Add the plantain, tomato and sweetcorn and cook for 5 minutes.

3 Add the tarragon, vegetable stock, chilli and salt and pepper and simmer for 10 minutes or until the plantain is tender. Stir in the nutmeg and serve at once.

Groundnut Soup

Groundnuts (or peanuts), are very widely used in sauces in African cooking. You'll find groundnut paste in health food shops – it makes a wonderfully rich soup, but you could use peanut butter instead if you prefer. Traditionally the okra are chopped, which gives the soup a slightly "tacky" consistency.

INGREDIENTS

Serves 4

45ml/3 tbsp pure groundnut paste
    or peanut butter
1.5 litres/2½ pints/6¼ cups stock
    or water
30ml/2 tbsp tomato purée
1 onion, chopped
2 slices fresh root ginger
1.5ml/¼ tsp dried thyme
1 bay leaf
salt and chilli powder
225g/8oz white yam, diced
10 small okras, trimmed (optional)

1 Place the groundnut paste or peanut butter in a bowl, add 300ml/½ pint/1¼ cups of the stock or water and the tomato purée and blend together to make a smooth paste.

2 Spoon the nut mixture into a saucepan and add the onion, ginger, thyme, bay leaf, salt, chilli and the remaining stock.

3 Heat gently until simmering, then cook for 1 hour, stirring from time to time to prevent the nut mixture sticking.

4 Add the white yam, cook for a further 10 minutes, and then add the okra, if using, and simmer until both are tender. Serve at once.

Chicken, Tomato and Christophene Soup

INGREDIENTS

Serves 4

225g/8oz skinless, boneless chicken
    breasts
1 garlic clove, crushed
pinch of freshly nutmeg
25g/1oz/2 tbsp butter or margarine
½ onion, finely chopped
15ml/1 tbsp tomato purée
400g/14oz can tomatoes, puréed
1.2 litres/2 pints/5 cups chicken stock
1 fresh chilli, seeded and chopped
1 christophene, peeled and diced,
    about 350g/12oz
5ml/1 tsp dried oregano
2.5ml/½ tsp dried thyme
50g/2oz smoked haddock fillet,
    skinned and diced
salt and freshly ground black pepper
fresh snipped chives, to garnish

1 Dice the chicken, place in a bowl and season with salt, pepper, garlic and nutmeg. Mix well to flavour the chicken and then set aside for about 30 minutes.

2 Melt the butter or margarine in a large saucepan, add the chicken and sauté over a moderate heat for 5–6 minutes. Stir in the onion and fry gently for a further 5 minutes until the onion is slightly softened.

3 Add the tomato purée, puréed tomatoes, stock, chilli, christophene and herbs. Bring to the boil, cover and simmer gently for 35 minutes until the christophene is tender.

4 Add the smoked fish, simmer for a further 5 minutes or until the fish is cooked through, adjust the seasoning and pour into warmed soup bowls. Garnish with a scattering of snipped chives and serve.

Vegetable Soup with Coconut

INGREDIENTS

Serves 4

½ red onion
175g/6oz each, turnip, sweet potato
   and pumpkin
30ml/2 tbsp butter or margarine
5ml/1 tsp dried marjoram
2.5ml/½ tsp ground ginger
1.5ml/¼ tsp ground cinnamon
15ml/1 tbsp chopped spring onion
1 litre/1¾ pint/4 cups well-flavoured
   vegetable stock
30ml/2 tbsp flaked almonds
1 fresh chilli, seeded and chopped
5ml/1 tsp sugar
25g/1oz creamed coconut
salt and freshly ground black pepper
chopped coriander, to garnish

1 Finely chop the onion, then peel the turnip, sweet potato and pumpkin and chop into medium-size dice.

2 Melt the butter or margarine in a large non-stick saucepan. Fry the onion for 4–5 minutes. Add the diced vegetables and fry for 3–4 minutes.

3 Add the marjoram, ginger, cinnamon, spring onion, salt and pepper. Fry over a low heat for about 10 minutes, stirring frequently.

4 Add the vegetable stock, flaked almonds, chopped chilli and sugar and stir well to mix, then cover and simmer gently for 10–15 minutes until the vegetables are just tender.

5 Grate the creamed coconut into the soup and stir to mix. Sprinkle with chopped coriander, if liked, spoon into warmed bowls and serve.

Yam Balls

Yam balls are a popular snack in many African countries. They are traditionally made quite plain, but can be flavoured with chopped vegetables and herbs, as in this recipe, or with cooked meat or fish, or spices.

INGREDIENTS

Makes about 24 balls
450g/1lb white yam
30ml/2 tbsp finely chopped onion
45ml/3 tbsp chopped tomatoes
2.5ml/½ tsp chopped fresh thyme
1 green chilli, finely chopped
15ml/1 tbsp finely chopped spring onion
1 garlic clove, crushed
1 egg, beaten
salt and freshly ground black pepper
oil, for shallow frying
seasoned flour, for dusting

1 Peel the yam, cut into pieces and boil in salted water for about 30 minutes until tender. Drain and mash.

2 Add the onion, tomatoes, thyme, chilli, spring onion, garlic, then stir in the egg and seasoning and mix well.

3 Using a dessertspoon, scoop a little of the mixture at a time and mould into balls. Heat a little oil in a large frying pan, roll the yam balls in the seasoned flour and then fry for a few minutes until golden brown. Drain the yam balls on kitchen paper and keep them warm while cooking the rest of the mixture. Serve hot.

> ——— COOK'S TIP ———
>
> If you like, add fresh chopped herbs to the yam mixture; parsley and chives make a good combination. Mix in 30ml/2 tbsp with the egg and seasoning.

Tatale

Overripe plantains are never thrown away and in Ghana they are often used to make this well-loved snack.

INGREDIENTS

Serves 4
2 overripe plantains
25–50g/1–2oz/2–4 tbsp self-raising flour
1 small onion, finely chopped
1 egg, beaten
5ml/1 tsp palm oil (optional)
salt
1 fresh green chilli, seeded and chopped
oil, for shallow frying

1 Peel and mash the plantains. Place in bowl and add enough flour to bind, stirring thoroughly.

2 Add the onion, egg, palm oil, if using, salt and chilli. Mix well and leave to stand for 20 minutes.

3 Heat a little oil in a large frying pan. Spoon dessertspoons of mixture into the pan and fry in batches for 3–4 minutes until golden, turning once. Drain the fritters on kitchen paper and serve hot or cold.

Spicy Kebabs

INGREDIENTS

Makes 18–20 balls

450g/1lb minced beef
1 egg
3 garlic cloves, crushed
½ onion, finely chopped
2.5ml/½ tsp freshly ground black
   pepper
7.5ml/1½ tsp ground cumin
7.5ml/1½ tsp dhania (ground
   coriander)
5ml/1 tsp ground ginger
10ml/2 tsp garam masala
15ml/1 tbsp lemon juice
50–75g/2–3oz/1–1½ cups fresh white
   breadcrumbs
1 small chilli, seeded and chopped
salt
oil, for deep frying

1 Place the minced beef in a large bowl and add the egg, garlic, onion, spices, seasoning, lemon juice, about 50g/1oz/1 cup of the breadcrumbs and the chilli.

2 Using your hands or a wooden spoon, mix the ingredients together until the mixture is firm. If it feels sticky, add more of the breadcrumbs and mix again until firm.

3 Heat the oil in a large heavy pan or deep-fat fryer. Shape the mixture into balls or fingers and fry, a few at a time, for 5 minutes or until well browned all over.

4 Using a slotted spoon, drain the kebabs and then transfer to a plate lined with kitchen paper. Cook the remaining kebabs in the same way and then serve, if you like, with Kachumbali or a spicy dip.

Assiette of Plantains

This melange of succulent sweet and savoury plantains makes a delicious crunchy appetizer.

INGREDIENTS

Serves 4

2 green plantains
1 yellow plantain
½ onion
pinch of garlic granules
salt and cayenne pepper
vegetable oil, for shallow frying

1 Heat the oil in a large frying pan over a moderate heat. While the oil is heating, peel one of the green plantains and cut into very thin rounds using a vegetable peeler.

2 Fry the plantain rounds in the oil for about 3 minutes, turning until golden brown. Drain on kitchen paper and keep warm.

3 Coarsely grate the other green plantain and put on a plate. Slice the onion into wafer-thin shreds and mix with the grated plantain.

4 Heat a little more oil in the frying pan and fry handfuls of the mixture for 2–3 minutes, until golden, turning once. Drain on kitchen paper and keep warm with the green plantain rounds.

5 Heat a little more oil in the frying pan and, while it is heating, peel the yellow plantain, cut in half lengthways and dice. Sprinkle with garlic granules and cayenne pepper and then fry in the hot oil until golden brown, turning to brown evenly. Drain on kitchen paper and then arrange the three varieties of cooked plantains in shallow dishes. Sprinkle with salt and serve as a snack.

Cameroon Suya

INGREDIENTS

Serves 4

450g/1lb frying steak
2.5ml/½ tsp sugar
5ml/1 tsp garlic granules
5ml/1 tsp ground ginger
5ml/1 tsp paprika
5ml/1 tsp ground cinnamon
pinch of chilli powder
10ml/2 tsp onion salt
50g/2oz/½ cup peanuts, finely crushed
vegetable oil, for brushing

1 Trim the steak of any fat and then cut into 2.5cm/1in wide strips. Place in a bowl or a shallow dish.

2 Mix the sugar, garlic granules, spices and onion salt together in a small bowl. Add the crushed peanuts and then scatter over the steak, mixing well so that the spices are worked into the meat.

3 Thread the steak on to six satay sticks, pushing the meat close together. Place in a shallow dish, cover loosely with foil and leave to marinate in a cool place for a few hours.

4 Preheat a grill or barbecue. Brush the meat with a little oil and then cook on a moderate heat for about 15 minutes, until evenly brown.

— COOK'S TIP —

If barbecueing the meat, try to avoid it cooking too quickly or burning.

Akkras

These fritters are almost always made from black-eyed beans. For a quicker version, after soaking the beans, drain them thoroughly and liquidize without removing the skins.

INGREDIENTS

Serves 4

250g/8oz/1¼ cups dried black-eyed beans
1 onion, chopped
1 red chilli, halved, with seeds removed (optional)
150ml/¼ pint/⅔ cup water
oil, for deep frying

1 Soak the black-eyed beans in plenty of cold water for 6–8 hours or overnight. Drain the beans and then, with a brisk action, rub the beans between the palms of your hands to remove the skins.

2 Return the beans to the bowl, top up with water and the skins will float to the surface. Discard the skins and soak the beans again for 2 hours.

3 Place the beans in a blender or food processor with the onion, chilli, if using, and a little water. Blend to make a thick paste. Pour the mixture into a large bowl and whisk for a few minutes.

4 Heat the oil in a large heavy saucepan and fry spoonfuls of the mixture for 4 minutes until golden brown.

Avocado and Smoked Fish Salad

Avocado and smoked fish make a good combination, and flavoured with herbs and spices, create a delectable salad.

INGREDIENTS

Serves 4
15g/½oz/1 tbsp butter or margarine
½ onion, finely sliced
5ml/1 tsp mustard seeds
225g/8oz smoked mackerel, flaked
30ml/2 tbsp coriander leaves, chopped
2 firm tomatoes, peeled and chopped
15ml/1 tbsp lemon juice

For the salad
2 avocados
½ cucumber
15ml/1 tbsp lemon juice
2 firm tomatoes
1 green chilli
salt and freshly ground black pepper

1 Melt the butter or margarine in a frying pan, add the onion and mustard seeds and fry for about 5 minutes until the onion is soft.

2 Add the fish, coriander leaves, tomatoes and lemon juice and cook over a low heat for 2–3 minutes. Remove from the heat and cool.

3 To make the salad, slice the avocados and cucumber thinly. Place together in a bowl and sprinkle with the lemon juice.

4 Slice the tomatoes and deseed and finely chop the chilli.

5 Place the fish mixture in the centre of a serving large plate.

6 Arrange the avocados, cucumber and tomatoes decoratively around the outside the fish. Alternatively, spoon a quarter of the fish mixture on to each of four serving plates and divide the avocados, cucumber and tomatoes equally. Sprinkle with the chopped chilli and a little salt and pepper and serve.

COOK'S TIP

Smoked mackerel has a distinctive flavour, but smoked haddock or cod can also be used in this salad, or a mixture of mackerel and haddock. For a speedy salad, canned tuna makes a convenient substitute.

King Prawns with Spicy Dip

The spicy dip served with this dish is equally good made from peanuts instead of cashew nuts. Vegetarians can enjoy this, too, if you make it with vegetables or tofu cubes. For a light meal, serve with boiled rice or bread.

INGREDIENTS

Serves 4–6

24 unshelled raw king prawns
juice of ½ lemon
5ml/1 tsp paprika
1 bay leaf
1 thyme sprig
salt and freshly ground black pepper
vegetable oil, for brushing

For the spicy dip
1 onion, chopped
4 canned plum tomatoes, plus 60ml/
  4 tbsp of the juice
½ green pepper, seeded and chopped
1 garlic clove, crushed
15ml/1 tbsp cashew nuts
15ml/1 tbsp soy sauce
15ml/1 tbsp dessicated coconut

1 Shell the prawns, leaving the tails on. Place in a shallow dish and sprinkle with the lemon juice, paprika and seasoning. Cover and chill.

2 Put the shells in a saucepan with the bay leaf and thyme, cover with water, and bring to the boil. Simmer for about 30 minutes, then strain the stock into a measuring jug. Top up with water, if necessary, to 300ml/ ½ pint/1¼ cups.

3 To make the spicy dip, place all the ingredients in a blender or food processor and blend until smooth.

4 Pour into a saucepan with the prawn stock and simmer over a moderate heat for 30 minutes, until the sauce is fairly thick.

5 Preheat a grill. Thread the prawns on to small skewers, then brush the prawns on both sides with a little oil and grill under a low heat until cooked, turning once. Serve with the dip for a starter. For a main course, omit the skewers, grill the prawns and pour the sauce over them.

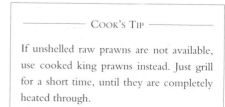

— COOK'S TIP —

If unshelled raw prawns are not available, use cooked king prawns instead. Just grill for a short time, until they are completely heated through.

Kofta Curry

Although fiddly, these koftas are well worth making. To save time, prepare in advance and chill until ready to cook.

INGREDIENTS

Serves 4

450g/1lb minced beef or lamb
45ml/3 tbsp finely chopped onion
15ml/1 tbsp chopped fresh coriander
15ml/1 tbsp natural yogurt
about 60ml/4 tbsp plain flour
10ml/2 tsp ground cumin
5ml/1 tsp garam masala
5ml/1 tsp ground turmeric
5ml/1 tsp dhania (ground coriander)
1 green chilli, seeded and finely
   chopped
2 garlic cloves, crushed
1.5ml/¼ tsp black mustard seeds
1 egg (optional)
salt and freshly ground black pepper

For the curry sauce
30ml/2 tbsp ghee or butter
1 onion, finely chopped
2 garlic cloves, crushed
45ml/3 tbsp curry powder
4 green cardamom pods
600ml/1 pint/2½ cups hot chicken
   stock or water
15ml/1 tbsp tomato purée
30ml/2 tbsp natural yogurt
15ml/1 tbsp chopped fresh coriander

1 Put the minced beef or lamb into a large bowl, add all the remaining meatball ingredients and mix well with your hands. Roll the mixture into small balls and put aside on a floured plate until required.

2 To make the curry sauce, heat the ghee or butter in a saucepan over a moderate heat and fry the onion and garlic for about 10 minutes until the onion is soft and buttery.

3 Reduce the heat and then add the curry powder and cardamon pods and cook for a few minutes, stirring well.

4 Slowly stir in the stock or water and then add the tomato purée, yogurt and coriander and stir well.

5 Simmer gently for 10 minutes. Add the koftas a few at a time, allow to cook briefly and then add a few more, until all of the koftas are in the pan. Simmer, uncovered, for about 20 minutes or until the koftas are cooked through. Avoid stirring, but gently shake the pan occasionally to move the koftas around. The curry should thicken slightly but if it becomes too dry, add a little more stock or water. Serve hot.

--- COOK'S TIP ---

Ghee is a form of clarified butter – it's made by heating butter until the water it contains has evaporated. The fat that remains can then be heated to high temperatures without burning. Ghee is widely used in Indian and Pakistani cooking and, because it is pre-cooked, has a distinctive flavour.

Lamb and Vegetable Pilau

INGREDIENTS

Serves 4

For the meat curry

450g/1lb boned shoulder of lamb,
  cubed
2.5ml/½ tsp dried thyme
2.5ml/½ tsp paprika
5ml/1 tsp garam masala
1 garlic clove, crushed
25ml/1½ tbsp vegetable oil
900ml/1½ pints/3¾ cups lamb stock
  or water
salt and freshly ground black pepper

For the rice

30ml/2 tbsp butter or margarine
1 onion, chopped
175g/6oz potato, diced
1 carrot, sliced
½ red pepper, seeded and chopped
115g/4oz green cabbage, sliced
1 green chilli, seeded and finely
  chopped
60ml/4 tbsp natural yogurt
2.5ml/½ tsp ground cumin
5 green cardamom pods
2 garlic cloves, crushed
350g/12oz/1½ cups basmati rice
about 50g/2oz/½ cup cashew nuts
salt and freshly ground black pepper

1 First make the meat curry. Place
the lamb in a large bowl and add
the thyme, paprika, garam masala,
garlic and salt and pepper. Stir well to
mix, then cover and set aside in a cool
place for 2–3 hours to marinate.

2 Heat the oil in a large saucepan and
fry the lamb, in batches if necessary,
over a moderate heat for 5–6 minutes,
until browned.

3 Add the stock or water, stir well
and then cook, covered, for 35–40
minutes or until the lamb is just tender.
Transfer the lamb to a plate or bowl
and pour the liquid into a measuring
jug, topping up with water if necessary,
to make 600ml/1 pint/2½ cups.

4 To make the rice, melt the butter
or margarine and fry the onion,
potato and carrot for 5 minutes.

5 Add the red pepper, cabbage, chilli,
yogurt, spices, garlic and the
reserved meat stock. Stir well, cover,
and then simmer gently for 5–10
minutes, until the cabbage has wilted.

6 Stir in the rice and lamb, cover
and simmer over a low heat for
20 minutes or until the rice is cooked.
Sprinkle in the cashew nuts and season
to taste with salt and freshly ground
black pepper. Serve hot.

COOK'S TIP

If you prefer, fewer vegetables can be used
for this dish and cubed chicken or minced
lamb substituted for the cubed lamb.
Basmati rice is ideal, but long grain rice
may be used instead. The amount of liquid
can be varied, depending on whether firm,
or well-cooked rice is preferred.

Beef in Aubergine Sauce

When served with boiled yam or rice, this makes a hearty dish.

INGREDIENTS

Serves 4

450g/1lb stewing beef
5ml/1 tsp dried thyme
45ml/3 tbsp palm or vegetable oil
1 large onion, finely chopped
2 garlic cloves, crushed
4 canned plum tomatoes, chopped, plus
    60ml/4 tbsp of the juice
15ml/1 tbsp tomato purée
2.5ml/$\frac{1}{2}$ tsp mixed spice
1 fresh red chilli, seeded and chopped
900ml/1$\frac{1}{2}$ pints/3$\frac{3}{4}$ cups chicken stock
    or water
1 large aubergine, about 350g/12oz
salt and freshly ground black pepper

1 Cut the beef into cubes and season with 2.5ml/$\frac{1}{2}$ tsp of the thyme and salt and pepper.

2 Heat 15ml/1 tbsp of the oil in a large saucepan and fry the meat, in batches if necessary, for 8–10 minutes until well browned. Transfer to a bowl using a slotted spoon and set aside.

3 Heat the remaining oil in the saucepan and fry the onion and garlic for a few minutes, then add the tomatoes and tomato juice and simmer for 5–10 minutes, stirring occasionally.

4 Add the tomato purée, mixed spice, chilli and remaining thyme, stir well, then add the reserved beef and the stock or water. Bring to the boil, cover and simmer gently for 30 minutes.

5 Cut the aubergine into 1cm/$\frac{1}{2}$ in dice. Stir into the beef mixture and cook, covered, for a further 30 minutes until the beef is completely tender. Adjust the seasoning and serve hot.

Mutton with Black-Eyed Beans and Pumpkin

Cooking meat together with vegetables, especially beans, is very common in African cooking. The pumpkin brings a lovely sweetness to this dish.

INGREDIENTS

Serves 4

450g/1lb boneless lean mutton or lamb, cubed
1 litre/1¾ pint/4 cups chicken or lamb stock or water
75g/3oz/½ cup black-eyed beans, soaked for 6 hours, or overnight
1 onion, chopped
2 garlic cloves, crushed
40ml/2½ tbsp tomato purée
7.5ml/1½ tsp dried thyme
7.5ml/1½ tsp palm or vegetable oil
5ml/1 tsp mixed spice
2.5ml/½ tsp freshly ground black pepper
115g/4oz pumpkin, chopped
salt and a little hot pepper sauce

1 Put the mutton or lamb in a large saucepan with the stock or water and bring to the boil. Skim off any foam, then reduce the heat, cover and simmer for 1 hour.

2 Stir in the drained black-eyed beans and continue cooking for about 35 minutes.

3 Add the onion, garlic, tomato purée, thyme, oil, mixed spice, black pepper and salt and hot pepper sauce and cook for a further 15 minutes or until the beans are tender.

4 Add the pumpkin and simmer for 10 minutes, until the pumpkin is very soft or almost mushy. Serve with boiled yam, plantains or sweet potatoes.

COOK'S TIP

Mutton is a mature meat with a very good flavour and texture, ideal for stews and casseroles. If mutton is not available, lamb makes a good substitute. Any dried white beans can be used instead of black-eyed beans. If a firmer texture is preferred, cook the pumpkin for about 5 minutes only, until just tender.

Spiced Fried Lamb

An Ethiopian dish, *Awaze Tibs*, flavoured with a red pepper spice mixture called *berbiri*, which is traditionally made from a variety of East African herbs and spices. This version uses spices that are a little easier to find!

INGREDIENTS

Serves 4

450g/1lb lamb fillet
45ml/3 tbsp olive oil
1 red onion, sliced
2.5ml/½ tsp grated fresh root ginger
2 garlic cloves, crushed
½ green chilli, seeded and finely chopped (optional)
15ml/ 1 tbsp clarified butter or ghee
salt and freshly ground black pepper

For the berbiri

2.5ml/½ tsp each chilli powder, paprika, ground ginger, ground cinnamon, ground cardamom seeds and dried basil
5ml/1 tsp garlic granules

1 To make the berbiri, combine all the ingredients in a small bowl and tip into an airtight container. Berberi will keep for several months if stored in a dry cool place.

2 Trim the meat of any fat and then cut into 2cm/¾ in cubes.

3 Heat the oil in a large frying pan and fry the meat and onion for 5–6 minutes, until the meat is browned on all sides.

4 Add the ginger and garlic to the pan and 10ml/2 tsp of the berbiri, then stir-fry over a brisk heat for a further 5–10 minutes.

5 Add the chilli, if using, and season well with salt and pepper. Just before serving, add the butter or ghee and stir well.

COOK'S TIP

Clarified butter is traditionally used for this recipe. It can be made by gently heating butter up to boiling point, preferably unsalted butter, and then scooping off the milk solids that rise to the surface.

Lamb Tagine with Coriander and Spices

Here is Rachida Mounti's version of a Moroccan-style tagine. It can be made with chops or cutlets, and either marinated or cooked immediately after seasoning.

INGREDIENTS

Serves 4

4 lamb chump chops
2 garlic cloves, crushed
pinch of saffron strands
2.5ml/½ tsp ground cinnamon, plus
   extra to garnish
2.5ml/½ tsp ground ginger
15ml/1 tbsp chopped fresh coriander
15ml/1 tbsp chopped fresh parsley
1 onion, finely chopped
45ml/3 tbsp olive oil
300ml/½ pint/1¼ cups lamb stock
50g/2oz/½ cup blanched almonds,
   to garnish
5ml/1 tsp sugar
salt and freshly ground black pepper

1 Season the lamb with the garlic, saffron, cinnamon, ginger and a little salt and black pepper. Place on a large plate and sprinkle with the coriander, parsley and onion. Cover loosely and set aside in the fridge for a few hours to marinate.

2 Heat the oil in a large frying pan, over a moderate heat. Add the marinated lamb and all the herbs and onion from the dish.

3 Fry for 1–2 minutes, turning once, then add the stock, bring to the boil and simmer gently for 30 minutes, turning the chops once.

4 Meanwhile, heat a small frying pan over a moderate heat, add the almonds and dry fry until golden, shaking the pan occasionally to ensure they colour evenly. Transfer to a bowl and set aside.

5 Transfer the chops to a serving plate and keep warm. Increase the heat under the pan and boil the sauce until reduced by about half. Stir in the sugar. Pour the sauce over the chops and sprinkle with the fried almonds and a little extra ground cinnamon.

COOK'S TIP

Lamb tagine is a fragrant dish, originating in North Africa. It is traditionally made in a cooking dish, known as a tagine, from where it takes its name. This dish consists of a plate with a tall lid with sloping sides. It has a narrow opening to let steam escape, while retaining the flavour.

Roast Lamb with Saffron and Tomato

A favourite roast for Sunday lunch. Boiled rice, root vegetables and fried plantain make delicious accompaniments.

INGREDIENTS

Serves 6
2 garlic cloves, crushed
15ml/1 tbsp finely chopped fresh mint
10ml/2 tsp ground cumin
5ml/1 tsp dried thyme
45ml/3 tbsp lemon juice
30ml/2 tbsp olive oil
1.5kg/3lb leg of lamb
lamb stock, for basting (optional)
salt and freshly ground black pepper

For the saffron and tomato sauce
30ml/2 tbsp vegetable oil
1 red onion, sliced
2 garlic cloves, crushed
400g/14oz can chopped tomatoes
10ml/2 tsp ground cinnamon
5ml/1 tsp dried tarragon
generous pinch of saffron threads
4 slices fresh root ginger
1 green chilli, seeded and finely chopped
600ml/1 pint/2½ cups lamb stock or water
salt and freshly ground black pepper

COOK'S TIP

African cooks almost always prefer to roast lamb until it is well done. If you like your meat a little pinker, then reduce the cooking time accordingly.

1 Mix together the garlic, mint, cumin, thyme, lemon juice, olive oil and salt and pepper. Cut three fairly deep slits into the lamb and rub the mixture all over the meat, pressing well into the slits. Cover loosely with clear film and leave to marinate overnight in the fridge.

2 Preheat the oven to 190°C/375°F/Gas 5. Place the lamb in a large roasting tin, cover with foil and roast for about 2 hours, basting occasionally with the pan juices or a little stock, if preferred.

3 Meanwhile make the sauce, heat the oil in a large saucepan and fry the onion and garlic over a moderate heat for 4–5 minutes until the onion is fairly soft.

4 Add the tomatoes, cinnamon, tarragon, saffron, ginger, chilli and seasoning. Stir well and cook, uncovered, for about 5 minutes.

5 Add the stock or water, bring back to the boil and then simmer for about 30 minutes until well reduced and fairly thick. Adjust the seasoning if necessary and then remove the pan from the heat.

6 Transfer the cooked lamb to a serving plate, cover with foil and leave to stand in a warm place for 5–10 minutes. Pour off the excess fat from the roasting tin, then add the meat juices to the sauce and reheat. Carve the lamb into thin slices and serve with the sauce accompanied by thick slices of fried plantain.

VARIATIONS

Saffron is expensive, but you can use turmeric as a substitute to give a golden yellow colour. A lean cut shoulder of lamb can be used instead of the leg of lamb.

East African Roast Chicken

INGREDIENTS

Serves 6

1.75kg/4–4½ lb chicken
30ml/2 tbsp softened butter, plus extra
   for basting
3 garlic cloves, crushed
5ml/1 tsp freshly ground black pepper
5ml/1 tsp ground turmeric
2.5ml/½ tsp ground cumin
5ml/1 tsp dried thyme
15ml/1 tbsp finely chopped fresh
   coriander
60ml/4 tbsp thick coconut milk
60ml/4 tbsp medium-dry sherry
5ml/1 tsp tomato purée
salt and chilli powder

1 Remove the giblets from the chicken, if necessary, rinse out the cavity and pat the skin dry.

2 Put the butter and all the remaining ingredients in a bowl and mix together well to form a thick paste.

3 Gently ease the skin of the chicken away from the flesh and rub generously with the herb and butter mixture. Rub more of the mixture over the skin, legs and wings of the chicken and into the neck cavity.

4 Place the chicken in a roasting tin, cover loosely with foil and marinate overnight in the fridge.

5 Preheat the oven to 190°C/375°F/ Gas 5. Cover the chicken with clean foil and roast for 1 hour, then turn the chicken over and baste with the pan juices. Cover again with foil and cook for 30 minutes.

6 Remove the foil and place the chicken breast-side up. Rub with a little extra butter and roast for a further 10–15 minutes until the meat juices run clear and the skin is golden brown. Serve with a rice dish or a salad.

Yassa Chicken

Senegalese cooks make wonderful Yassa. Instead of frying, they often grill the chicken before adding it to the sauce. For a less tangy flavour, you can add less lemon juice, although it does mellow after cooking.

INGREDIENTS

Serves 4

150ml/¼ pint/⅔ cup lemon juice
60ml/4 tbsp malt vinegar
3 onions, sliced
60ml/4 tbsp groundnut or vegetable oil
1kg/2¼ lb chicken pieces
1 sprig thyme
1 green chilli, seeded and finely chopped
2 bay leaves
425ml/¾ pint/1⅞ cups chicken stock

1 Mix the lemon juice, vinegar, onions and 30ml/2 tbsp of the oil together, place the chicken pieces in a shallow dish and pour over the lemon mixture. Cover with clear film and leave to marinate for 3 hours.

2 Heat the remaining oil in a large saucepan and fry the chicken pieces for 4–5 minutes until browned.

3 Add the marinated onions to the chicken. Fry for 3 minutes, then add the marinade, thyme, chilli, bay leaves and half the stock.

4 Cover the pan and simmer gently over a moderate heat for about 35 minutes, until the chicken is cooked through, adding more stock as the sauce evaporates. Serve hot.

Joloff Chicken and Rice

Serve this well-known, colourful West African dish at a dinner party or other special occasion.

INGREDIENTS

Serves 4

1kg/2¼ lb chicken, cut into 4–6 pieces
2 garlic cloves, crushed
5ml/1 tsp dried thyme
30ml/ 2 tbsp palm or vegetable oil
400g/14oz can chopped tomatoes
15ml/1 tbsp tomato purée
1 onion, chopped
450ml/¾ pint/scant 2 cups chicken
    stock or water
30ml/2 tbsp dried shrimps or crayfish,
    ground
1 green chilli, seeded and finely
    chopped
350g/12oz/1½ cups long grain rice,
    washed

1 Rub the chicken with the garlic and thyme and set aside.

2 Heat the oil in a saucepan until hot but not smoking and brown the chicken pieces. Add the chopped tomatoes, tomato purée and onion. Cook over a moderately high heat for about 5 minutes, stirring occasionally at first and then more frequently as the tomatoes thicken.

3 Add the stock to the tomatoes and chicken and stir well. Bring to the boil, then reduce the heat, cover the pan and simmer for about 40 minutes. Add the shrimps or crayfish and the chilli. Simmer for a further 5 minutes, stirring occasionally.

4 Put the rice in a pan. Scoop 300ml/ ½ pint/1¼ cups of sauce into a jug, top up with water to 450ml/¾ pint/scant 2 cups and add to the rice. Cook for 10 minutes to partly absorb the liquid.

5 Place a piece of foil on top of the rice, cover and cook over a low heat for 10 minutes, adding a little more water if necessary. Transfer the chicken pieces to a serving plate. Simmer the sauce until reduced by half. Pour over the chicken and serve with the rice.

Chicken with Lentils

Kuku, this delicious tangy chicken stew, comes from Kenya. The amount of lemon juice can be reduced, if you would prefer a less sharp sauce.

INGREDIENTS

Serves 4–6

6 chicken thighs or pieces
2.5–4ml/ ^{1}/$_2$–^{3}/$_4$ tsp ground ginger
50g/2oz mung beans
60ml/4 tbsp corn oil
2 onions, finely chopped
2 garlic cloves, crushed
5 tomatoes, peeled and chopped
1 green chilli, seeded and finely
    chopped
30ml/2 tbsp lemon juice
300ml/^{1}/$_2$ pint/1^1/$_4$ cups coconut milk
300ml/^{1}/$_2$ pint/1^1/$_4$ cups water
15ml/1 tbsp chopped fresh coriander
salt and freshly ground black pepper

1 Season the chicken pieces with the ginger and a little salt and pepper and set aside in a cool place to marinate. Meanwhile, boil the mung beans in plenty of water for 35 minutes until soft, then mash well.

2 Heat the oil in a large saucepan over a moderate heat and fry the chicken pieces, in batches if necessary, until evenly browned. Transfer to a plate and set aside, reserving the oil and chicken juices in the pan.

3 In the same pan, fry the onions and garlic for 5 minutes, then add the tomatoes and chilli and cook for a further 1–2 minutes, stirring well.

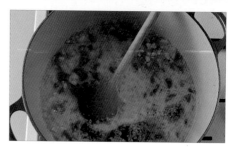

4 Add the mashed mung beans, lemon juice and coconut milk to the pan. Simmer for 5 minutes, then add the chicken pieces and a little water if the sauce is too thick. Stir in the coriander and simmer for about 35 minutes until the chicken is cooked through. Serve with a green vegetable and rice or chapatis.

Palava Chicken

This is a variation of the popular sauce from Ghana, which was originally made from fish. In Sierra Leone, peanut butter is often added, as in this version.

INGREDIENTS

Serves 4

675g/1½lb skinless, boneless chicken breasts
2 garlic cloves, crushed
30ml/2 tbsp butter or margarine
30ml/2 tbsp palm or vegetable oil
1 onion, finely chopped
4 tomatoes, peeled and chopped
30ml/2 tbsp peanut butter
600ml/1 pint/2½ cups chicken stock or water
1 thyme sprig or 5ml/1 tsp dried thyme
225g/8oz frozen leaf spinach, defrosted and chopped
1 fresh chilli, seeded and chopped
salt and freshly ground black pepper

1 Cut the chicken breasts into thin slices, place in a bowl and stir in the garlic and a little salt and pepper. Melt the butter or margarine in a large frying pan and fry the chicken over a moderate heat, turning once or twice to brown evenly. Transfer to a plate with a slotted spoon and set aside.

2 Heat the oil in a large saucepan and fry the onion and tomatoes over a high heat for 5 minutes until soft.

3 Reduce the heat, add the peanut butter and half of the stock or water and blend together well.

4 Cook for 4–5 minutes, stirring all the time to prevent the peanut butter burning, then add the remaining stock or water, thyme, spinach, chilli and seasoning. Stir in the chicken slices and cook over a moderate heat for about 10–15 minutes until the chicken is cooked through.

5 Pour into a warmed serving dish and serve with boiled yams, rice or ground rice.

COOK'S TIP

If you're short of time, frozen spinach is more convenient, but chopped fresh spinach, adds a fresher flavour to this recipe. Egusi – ground melon seed can be used instead of peanut butter.

Duck with Sherry and Pumpkin

INGREDIENTS

Serves 6

1 whole duck, about 1.75kg/4–4¹/₂lb
1 lemon
5ml/1 tsp garlic granules or 2 garlic
  cloves, crushed
5ml/1 tsp curry powder
2.5ml/¹/₂ tsp paprika
4ml/³/₄ tsp five-spice powder
30ml/2 tbsp soy sauce
salt and freshly ground black pepper
vegetable oil, for frying

For the sauce

75g/3oz pumpkin
1 onion, chopped
4 canned plum tomatoes
300ml/¹/₂ pint/1¹/₄ cups medium-dry
  sherry
about 300ml/¹/₂ pint/1¹/₄ cups water

1 Cut the duck into 10 pieces and place in a large bowl. Halve the lemon and squeeze the juice all over the duck and set aside.

2 In a small bowl, mix together the garlic, curry powder, paprika, five-spice powder and salt and pepper and rub into each of the duck pieces.

3 Sprinkle the duck with the soy sauce, cover loosely with clear film and leave to marinate overnight.

4 To make the sauce, cook the pumpkin in boiling water until tender, then blend to a purée with the onion and tomatoes.

— COOK'S TIP —

The back and wings of the duck are rather bony, so try and use just the fleshier parts or buy leg or breast portions.

---

5 Pat the duck pieces dry with kitchen paper, then heat a little oil in a wok or large frying pan and fry the duck for 15 minutes until crisp and brown. Set aside on a plate.

6 Wipe away the excess oil from the wok or frying pan with kitchen paper and pour in the pumpkin purée. Add the sherry and a little of the water, then bring to the boil and add the fried duck. Simmer for about 1 hour until the duck is cooked, adding more water if the sauce becomes too thick. Serve hot and hand soy sauce separately.

Stuffed Turkey Fillets in Lemon Sauce

Sweet potatoes and prawns flavoured with herbs and chilli make an unusual stuffing for turkey fillets. Reduce the amount of fresh chilli, if you prefer your food less hot.

INGREDIENTS

Serves 4

175g/6oz sweet potato
1 onion, finely chopped
5ml/1 tsp dried tarragon, crushed
2.5ml/½ tsp dried basil
1 green chilli, seeded and finely
   chopped
1 garlic clove, crushed
2.5ml/½ tsp dried thyme
2.5ml/½ tsp freshly ground black pepper
115g/4oz cooked, peeled prawns,
   chopped
4 turkey fillets, about 225g/8oz each
salt and freshly ground black pepper

For the lemon sauce
15ml/1 tbsp olive oil
½ onion, finely chopped
2 garlic cloves, crushed
300ml/½ pint/1¼ cups well-flavoured
   chicken stock
4ml/¾ tsp dried thyme
2.5ml/½ tsp dried basil
30ml/2 tbsp finely chopped fresh
   parsley
freshly ground black pepper
30ml/2 tbsp lemon juice

1 Preheat the oven to 180°C/350°F/ Gas 4. Cook the sweet potato in boiling water until tender, then drain, transfer to a bowl and mash until smooth.

2 Add the onion, tarragon, basil, chilli, garlic clove, thyme, black pepper and prawns and mix well.

COOK'S TIP

If you prefer smaller fillets, use chicken instead of turkey, and reduce the cooking time in the oven by about half.

3 Lay the turkey fillets on a plate and season with salt and little extra black pepper. Place a little of the sweet potato stuffing in the centre of each fillet, fold over the sides and roll up. Secure with a wooden cocktail stick, if necessary, and place in a buttered ovenproof dish, seam-side down.

4 To make the lemon sauce, heat the olive oil in a frying pan over a moderate heat and fry the onion and garlic for 5–7 minutes, until soft, stirring frequently. Stir in the stock and simmer for a few minutes.

5 Stir in the thyme, basil, parsley, pepper and lemon juice and simmer for 2 minutes, then pour the sauce around the turkey, cover with foil and bake in the oven for about 1½ hours until the turkey is cooked, basting frequently with the sauce to keep the rolls moist. Serve with root vegetables, bulgur wheat or rice.

FISH
AND
SEAFOOD

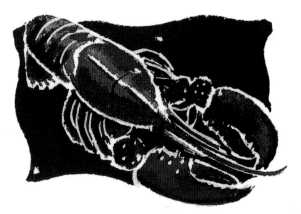

African waters are teeming with interesting and tasty fish and shellfish – from the humble mackerel to the fabulous lobster. There are more than 200 types of fish in Nigeria alone! For those who live around the coast or by lakes or rivers, fresh fish can be found in abundance and there are a huge number of superb fish dishes, like Fish and Prawns with Spinach, and Coconut and Fish with Crab Meat and Aubergine, which have been adapted to use fish easily available in this country. Other recipes, like Tanzanian Fish Curry or Baked Red Snapper, use fish that are increasingly available in larger supermarkets, and are well worth looking out for.

Fish and Prawns with Spinach and Coconut

INGREDIENTS

Serves 4

450g/1lb white fish fillets (cod or
  haddock)
15ml/1 tbsp lemon or lime juice
2.5ml/½ tsp garlic granules
5ml/1 tsp ground cinnamon
2.5ml/½ tsp dried thyme
2.5ml/½ paprika
2.5ml/½ tsp freshly ground black
  pepper
seasoned flour, for dusting
vegetable oil, for shallow frying
salt

For the sauce

25g/1oz/2 tbsp butter or margarine
1 onion, finely chopped
1 garlic clove, crushed
300ml/½ pint/1¼ cups coconut milk
115g/4oz fresh spinach, finely sliced
225–275g/8–10oz cooked, peeled
  prawns
1 red chilli, seeded and finely chopped

1 Place the fish fillets in a shallow
bowl and sprinkle with the lemon
or lime juice.

2 Blend together the garlic granules,
cinnamon, thyme, paprika, pepper
and salt and sprinkle over the fish.
Cover loosely with clear film and leave
to marinate in a cool place or
refrigerator for a few hours.

3 Meanwhile, make the sauce. Melt
the butter or margarine in a large
saucepan and fry the onion and garlic
for 5–6 minutes, until the onion is soft,
stirring frequently.

4 Place the coconut milk and spinach
in a separate saucepan and bring to
the boil. Cook gently for a few minutes
until the spinach has wilted and the
coconut milk has reduced a little, then
set aside to cool slightly.

5 Blend the spinach mixture in a
blender or food processor for 30
seconds and add to the onion with the
prawns and red chilli. Stir well and
simmer gently for a few minutes then
set aside while cooking the fish.

6 Cut the marinated fish into
5cm/2in pieces and dip in the
seasoned flour. Heat a little oil in a
large frying pan and fry the fish pieces,
in batches if necessary, for 2–3 minutes
each side until golden brown. Drain on
kitchen paper.

7 Arrange the fish on a warmed
serving plate. Gently reheat the
sauce and serve separately in a sauce
boat or poured over the fish.

Tanzanian Fish Curry

INGREDIENTS

Serves 2–3

1 large snapper or red bream
1 lemon
45ml/3 tbsp vegetable oil
1 onion, finely chopped
2 garlic cloves, crushed
45ml/3 tbsp curry powder
400g/14oz can chopped tomatoes
20ml/1 heaped tbsp smooth peanut
   butter, preferably unsalted
½ green pepper, chopped
2 slices fresh root ginger
1 green chilli, seeded and finely
   chopped
about 600ml/1 pint/2½ cups fish stock
15ml/1 tbsp finely chopped fresh
   coriander
salt and freshly ground black pepper

1 Season the fish, inside and out with salt and pepper and place in a shallow bowl. Halve the lemon and squeeze the juice all over the fish. Cover loosely with clear film and leave to marinate for at least 2 hours.

2 Heat the oil in a large saucepan and fry the onion and garlic for 5–6 minutes until soft. Reduce the heat, add the curry powder and cook, stirring for a further 5 minutes.

3 Stir in the tomatoes and then the peanut butter, mixing well, then add the green pepper, ginger, chilli and stock. Stir well and simmer gently for 10 minutes.

COOK'S TIP

The fish can be fried before adding to the sauce, if preferred. Dip in seasoned flour and fry in oil in a pan or a wok for a few minutes before adding to the sauce.

4 Cut the fish into pieces and gently lower into the sauce. Simmer for a further 20 minutes or until the fish is cooked, then using a slotted spoon, transfer the fish pieces to a plate.

5 Stir the coriander into the sauce and adjust the seasoning. If the sauce is very thick, add a little extra stock or water. Return the fish to the sauce, cook gently to heat through and then serve immediately.

Fish with Crab Meat and Aubergine

Any filleted fish can be used in
this dish, cod, haddock or halibut
would all make good substitutes.
For a change, use peeled prawns
instead of the crabmeat.

INGREDIENTS

Serves 4

450–675g/1–1½lb salmon fillet,
  skinned and cut into 4 pieces
2 garlic cloves, crushed
juice of ½ lemon
15ml/1 tbsp vegetable oil
15g/½oz/1 tbsp butter or margarine
1 onion, cut into rings
175g/6oz fresh or canned crabmeat
salt and freshly ground black pepper

For the aubergine sauce

25g/1oz/2 tbsp butter or margarine
30ml/2 tbsp chopped spring onion
2 tomatoes, peeled and chopped
½ red pepper, seeded and finely
  chopped
1 large aubergine, peeled and chopped
450ml/¾ pint/1⅞ cups fish or vegetable
  stock
salt and freshly ground black pepper

1 Place the salmon fillet in a shallow
dish, season with the garlic and a
little salt and pepper. Sprinkle with the
lemon juice and set aside, covered, to
marinate for at least 1 hour.

2 Meanwhile, make the aubergine
sauce. Melt the butter or margarine
in a saucepan and gently fry the spring
onion and tomatoes for 5 minutes.

3 Add the red pepper and aubergine,
stir together and then add 300ml/
½ pint/1¼ cups of the stock. Simmer for
20 minutes until the aubergines are
mushy and the liquid has been absorbed
and then mash together well with a fork.

4 To cook the salmon, heat the oil
and butter or margarine in a large
frying pan. When the butter has
melted, scatter the onion rings over the
bottom of the pan and lay the salmon
pieces on top. Cover each piece of
salmon with crabmeat and then spoon
the aubergine mixture on top.

5 Pour the remaining stock around
the salmon, cover with a lid and
steam over a low to moderate heat until
the salmon is cooked through and flakes
easily when tested with a knife. The
sauce should be thick and fairly dry.

6 Arrange the fish on warmed
serving plates, spoon extra sauce
over and serve at once.

COOK'S TIP

Use a fish slice to carefully transfer the
salmon fillet to serving plates, to prevent
breaking up the fish.

Baked Red Snapper

Ingredients

Serves 3–4

1 large red snapper, cleaned
juice of 1 lemon
2.5ml/¹/₂ tsp paprika
2.5ml/¹/₂ tsp garlic granules
2.5ml/¹/₂ tsp dried thyme
2.5ml/¹/₂ tsp freshly ground black
  pepper

For the sauce

30ml/2 tbsp palm or vegetable oil
1 onion
400g/14oz can chopped tomatoes
2 garlic cloves
1 thyme sprig or 2.5ml/¹/₂ tsp dried
  thyme
1 green chilli, seeded and finely
  chopped
¹/₂ green pepper, seeded and chopped
300ml/¹/₂ pint/1¹/₄ cups fish stock
  or water

1 Preheat the oven to 200°C/
400°F/Gas 6 and then prepare the
sauce. Heat the oil in a saucepan, fry
the onion for 5 minutes, then add the
tomatoes, garlic, thyme and chilli.

— Cook's Tip —

If you prefer less sauce, remove the foil
after 20 minutes and continue baking
uncovered, until cooked.

2 Add the pepper and stock or water.
Bring to the boil, stirring, then
reduce the heat and simmer, covered,
for about 10 minutes until the
vegetables are soft. Leave to cool a little
and then place in a blender or food
processor and blend to a purée.

3 Wash the fish well and then score
the skin with a sharp knife in a
criss-cross pattern. Mix together the
lemon juice, paprika, garlic, thyme and
black pepper, spoon over the fish and
rub in well.

4 Place the fish in a greased baking
dish and pour the sauce over the
top. Cover with foil and bake for about
30–40 minutes or until the fish is
cooked and flakes easily when tested
with a knife. Serve with boiled rice.

Fish with Lemon, Red Onions and Coriander

INGREDIENTS

Serves 4

4 halibut or cod steaks or cutlets, about
  175g/6oz each
juice of 1 lemon
5ml/1 tsp garlic granules
5ml/1 tsp paprika
5ml/1 tsp ground cumin
4ml/¾ tsp dried tarragon
about 60ml/4 tbsp olive oil
flour, for dusting
300ml/½ pint/1¼ cups fish stock
2 red chillies, seeded and finely
  chopped
30ml/2 tbsp chopped fresh coriander
1 red onion, cut into rings
salt and freshly ground black pepper

1 Place the fish in a shallow bowl and mix together the lemon juice, garlic, paprika, cumin, tarragon and a little salt and pepper. Spoon over the lemon mixture, cover loosely with clear film and allow to marinate for a few hours or overnight in the fridge.

3 Pour the fish stock around the fish, and simmer, covered for about 5 minutes until the fish is thoroughly cooked through.

5 Transfer the fish and sauce to a serving plate and keep warm.

2 Gently heat all of the oil in a large non-stick frying pan, dust the fish with flour and then fry the fish for a few minutes each side, until golden brown all over.

4 Add the chopped red chillies and 15ml/1 tbsp of the coriander to the pan. Simmer for 5 minutes.

6 Wipe the pan, heat some olive oil and stir fry the onion rings until speckled brown. Scatter over the fish with the remaining chopped coriander and serve at once.

King Prawns in Almond Sauce

INGREDIENTS

Serves 4

450g/1lb raw king prawns
600ml/1 pint/2½ cups water
3 thin slices fresh root ginger
10ml/2 tsp curry powder
2 garlic cloves, crushed
15g/½ oz/1 tbsp butter or margarine
60ml/4 tbsp ground almonds
1 green chilli, seeded and finely
　chopped
45ml/3 tbsp single cream
salt and freshly ground black pepper

For the vegetables

15ml/1 tbsp mustard oil
15ml/1 tbsp vegetable oil
1 onion, sliced
½ red pepper, seeded and thinly sliced
½ green pepper, seeded and thinly
　sliced
1 christophene, peeled, stoned and cut
　into strips
salt and freshly ground black pepper

1 Shell the prawns and place shells in a saucepan with the water and ginger. Simmer, uncovered, for 15 minutes until reduced by half. Strain into a jug and discard the shells.

2 Devein the prawns, place in a bowl and season with the curry powder, garlic and salt and pepper and set aside.

3 Heat the mustard and vegetable oils in a large frying pan, add all the vegetables and stir fry for 5 minutes. Season with salt and pepper, spoon into a serving dish and keep warm.

4 Wipe out the frying pan, then melt the butter or margarine and sauté the prawns for about 5 minutes until pink. Spoon over the bed of vegetables, cover and keep warm.

5 Add the ground almonds and chilli to the pan, stir fry for a few seconds and then add the reserved stock and bring to the boil. Reduce the heat, stir in the cream and simmer for a few minutes, without boiling.

6 Pour the sauce over the vegetables and prawns before serving.

Fried Pomfret in Coconut Sauce

INGREDIENTS

Serves 4

4 medium pomfret
juice of 1 lemon
5ml/1 tsp garlic granules
salt and freshly ground black pepper
vegetable oil, for shallow frying

For the coconut sauce

450ml/¾ pint/1⅞ cups water
2 thin slices fresh root ginger
25–40g/1–1½ oz creamed coconut
30ml/2 tbsp vegetable oil
1 red onion, sliced
2 garlic cloves, crushed
1 green chilli, seeded and thinly sliced
15ml/1 tbsp chopped fresh coriander
salt and freshly ground black pepper

1 Cut the fish in half and sprinkle inside and out with the lemon juice. Season with the garlic granules and salt and pepper and set aside to marinate for a few hours.

2 Heat a little oil in a large frying pan. Pat away the excess lemon juice from the fish, fry in the oil for 10 minutes, turning once. Set aside.

3 To make the sauce, place the water in a saucepan with the slices of ginger, bring to the boil and simmer until the liquid is reduced to just over 300ml/½ pint/1¼ cups. Take out the ginger and reserve, then add the creamed coconut to the pan and stir until the coconut has melted.

4 Heat the oil in a wok or large pan and fry the onion and garlic for 2–3 minutes. Add the reserved ginger and coconut stock, the chilli and coriander, stir well and then gently add the fish. Simmer for 10 minutes, until the fish is cooked through. Transfer the fish to a warmed serving plate, adjust the seasoning for the sauce and pour over the fish. Serve immediately.

Donu's Lobster Piri Piri

Lobster in its shell, in true Nigerian style, flavoured with dried shrimp.

INGREDIENTS

Serves 2–4
2 cooked lobsters, halved
fresh coriander sprigs, to garnish

For the piri piri sauce
60ml/4 tbsp vegetable oil
2 onions, chopped
5ml/1 tsp chopped fresh root ginger
450g/1lb fresh or canned tomatoes, chopped
15ml/1 tbsp tomato purée
225g/8oz cooked, peeled prawns
10ml/2 tsp ground coriander
1 green chilli, seeded and chopped
15ml/1 tbsp ground dried shrimps or crayfish
600ml/1 pint/2½ cups water
1 green pepper, seeded and sliced
salt and freshly ground black pepper

1 Heat the oil in a large flameproof casserole and fry the onions, ginger, tomatoes and tomato purée for 5 minutes or until the onions are soft.

2 Add the prawns, ground coriander, chilli and ground shrimps or crayfish and stir well to mix.

3 Stir in the water, green pepper and salt and pepper, bring to the boil and simmer, uncovered, over a moderate heat for about 20–30 minutes until the sauce is reduced.

4 Add the lobsters to the sauce and cook for a few minutes to heat through. Arrange the lobster halves on warmed serving plates and pour the sauce over each one. Garnish with coriander sprigs and serve with fluffy white rice.

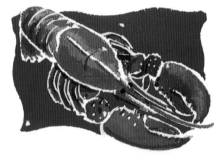

Tilapia in Turmeric, Mango and Tomato Sauce

Tilapia is widely used in African cooking, but can be found in most fishmongers. Yam or boiled yellow plantains are good accompaniments.

INGREDIENTS

Serves 4

4 tilapia
½ lemon
2 garlic cloves, crushed
2.5ml/½ tsp dried thyme
30ml/2 tbsp chopped spring onions
vegetable oil, for shallow frying
flour, for dusting
30ml/2 tbsp groundnut oil
15g/½ oz/1 tbsp butter or margarine
1 onion, finely chopped
3 tomatoes, peeled and finely chopped
5ml/1 tsp ground turmeric
60ml/4 tbsp white wine
1 green chilli, seeded and finely chopped
600ml/1 pint/2½ cups well-flavoured fish stock
5ml/1 tsp sugar
1 medium underripe mango, peeled and diced
15ml/1 tbsp chopped fresh parsley
salt and freshly ground black pepper

2 Heat a little vegetable oil in a large frying pan, coat the fish with some flour, then fry the fish on both sides for a few minutes until golden brown. Remove with a slotted spoon to a plate and set aside.

4 Add the turmeric, white wine, chilli, fish stock and sugar, stir well and bring to the boil, then simmer gently, covered, for 10 minutes.

5 Add the fish and cook over a gentle heat for about 15–20 minutes, until the fish is cooked through. Add the mango, arranging it around the fish, and cook briefly for 1–2 minutes to heat through.

1 Place the fish in a shallow bowl, squeeze the lemon juice all over the fish and gently rub in the garlic, thyme and some salt and pepper. Place some of the spring onion in the cavity of each fish, cover loosely with clear film and leave to marinate for a few hours or overnight in the fridge.

3 Heat the groundnut oil and butter or margarine in a saucepan and fry the onion for 4–5 minutes, until soft. Stir in the tomatoes and cook briskly for a few minutes.

6 Arrange the fish on a warmed serving plate with the mango and tomato sauce poured over. Garnish with chopped parsley and serve immediately.

VEGETABLE AND VEGETARIAN DISHES

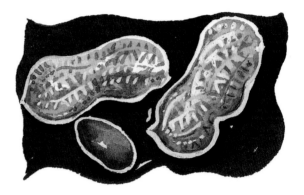

African cooks prepare lots of recipes using
vegetables and pulses, and for many people these
are the mainstay of their diet. Herbs and spices
add an extra dimension to these dishes, frequently
served with unusual and often fiery sauces.
Whether you are cooking a vegetarian meal, or
just want an interesting vegetable side dish, do
look out for the more unusual root and green
vegetables that are now available. Plantains, yams
and sweet potatoes are some of the typical
vegetables that make superb dishes. Other more
common vegetables, such as pumpkin and
sweetcorn, can, given the African treatment, be
transformed into tempting mouth-watering dishes.

Sese Plantain and Yam

INGREDIENTS

Serves 4

2 green plantains
450g/1lb white yam
2 tomatoes, peeled and chopped
1 red chilli, seeded and chopped
1 onion, chopped
½ vegetable stock cube
15ml/1 tbsp palm oil
15ml/1 tbsp tomato purée
salt

2 Place the plantains and yam in a large saucepan with 600ml/
1 pint/2½ cups water, bring to the boil and cook for 5 minutes. Add the tomatoes, chilli and onion and simmer for a further 10 minutes, then crumble in half the vegetable stock cube, stir well, cover and simmer for 5 minutes.

3 Stir in the oil and tomato purée and continue cooking for about
5 minutes until the plantains are tender. Season with salt and pour into a warmed serving dish. Serve immediately.

COOK'S TIP

To peel the plantains, cut in half, slit the plantains along the natural ridges, then lift off the skin in sections.

1 Peel the plantains and cut into six rounds, then peel and dice the yam.

Makande

A traditional dish from Uparie-Tanzania, which can be served with meat, fish or simply a salad.

INGREDIENTS

Serves 3–4

225g/8oz/1¼ cups red kidney beans, soaked overnight
1 onion, chopped
2 garlic cloves, crushed
75g/3oz creamed coconut
225g/8oz/1⅓ cups frozen sweetcorn
300ml/½ pint/1¼ cups vegetable stock or water
salt and freshly ground black pepper

1 Drain the kidney beans and place in a saucepan, cover with water and boil rapidly for 15 minutes. Reduce the heat and continue boiling for about 1 hour, until the beans are tender, adding more water if necessary. Drain, discarding the cooking liquid.

2 Place the beans in a clean pan with the onion, garlic, coconut, sweetcorn and salt and pepper.

3 Add the stock or water, bring to the boil and simmer for 20 minutes, stirring occasionally to dissolve the coconut.

4 Adjust the seasoning and spoon into a warmed serving dish. Serve with an onion and tomato salad.

Egusi Spinach and Egg

This is a superbly balanced dish for those who don't eat meat. Egusi, or ground melon seed, is widely used in West African cooking, adding a creamy texture and a nutty flavour to many recipes. It is especially good with fresh spinach.

INGREDIENTS

Serves 4
900g/2lb fresh spinach
115g/4oz ground egusi
90ml/6 tbsp groundnut or vegetable oil
4 tomatoes, peeled and chopped
1 onion, chopped
2 garlic cloves, crushed
1 slice fresh root ginger, finely chopped
150ml/¼ pint/⅔ cup vegetable stock
1 red chilli, seeded and finely chopped
6 eggs
salt

1 Roll the spinach into bundles and cut into strips. Place in a bowl.

2 Cover with boiling water, then drain through a sieve. Press with your fingers to remove excess water.

3 Place the egusi in a bowl and gradually add enough water to form a paste, stirring all the time.

4 Heat the oil in a saucepan, add the tomatoes, onion, garlic and ginger and fry over a moderate heat for about 10 minutes, stirring frequently.

5 Add the egusi paste, stock, chilli and salt, cook for 10 minutes, then add the spinach and stir into the sauce. Cook for 15 minutes, uncovered, stirring frequently.

6 Meanwhile hard-boil the eggs, stand in cold water for a few minutes to cool and then shell and cut in half. Arrange in a shallow serving dish and pour the egusi spinach over the top. Serve hot.

COOK'S TIP

Instead of using boiled eggs, you could make an omlette flavoured with herbs and garlic. Serve it either whole, or sliced, with the egusi sauce. If you can't find egusi, use ground almonds as a substitute.

Bean and Gari Loaf

This recipe is a newly created vegetarian dish using typical Ghanaian flavours and ingredients.

INGREDIENTS

Serves 4

225g/8oz/1¼ cups red kidney beans, soaked overnight
15g/½ oz/1 tbsp butter or margarine
1 onion, finely chopped
2 garlic cloves, crushed
½ red pepper, seeded and chopped
½ green pepper, seeded and chopped
1 green chilli, seeded and finely chopped
5ml/1 tsp mixed herbs
2 eggs
15ml/1 tbsp lemon juice
75ml/5 tbsp gari
salt and freshly ground black pepper

1 Drain the kidney beans, then place in a saucepan, cover with water and boil rapidly for 15 minutes. Reduce the heat and continue boiling for about 1 hour, until the beans are tender, adding more water if necessary. Drain, reserving the cooking liquid. Preheat the oven to 190°C/375°F/Gas 5 and grease a 900g/2lb loaf tin.

2 Melt the butter or margarine in a large frying pan and fry the onion, garlic and peppers for 5 minutes, then add the chilli, mixed herbs and a little salt and pepper.

3 Place the cooked kidney beans in a large bowl or in a food processor and mash or process to a pulp. Add the onion and pepper mixture and stir well to mix. Cool slightly, then stir in the eggs and lemon juice.

4 Place the gari in a separate bowl and sprinkle generously with warm water. The gari should become soft and fluffy after about 5 minutes.

5 Pour the gari into the bean and onion mixture and stir together thoroughly. If the consistency is too stiff, add a little of the bean liquid. Spoon the mixture into the prepared loaf tin and bake in the oven for 35–45 minutes, until firm to the touch.

6 Cool the loaf in the tin and then turn out on to a plate. Cut into thick slices and serve.

COOK'S TIP

Gari is a course-grained flour, used as a staple food, in a similar way to ground rice. It is made from a starchy root vegetable; cassava, which is first dried, then ground.

Vegetables in Peanut Sauce

INGREDIENTS

Serves 4

15ml/1 tbsp palm or vegetable oil
1 onion, chopped
2 garlic cloves, crushed
400g/14oz can tomatoes, puréed
45ml/3 tbsp smooth peanut butter,
  preferably unsalted
750ml/1¼ pint/3⅔ cups water
5ml/1 tsp dried thyme
1 green chilli, seeded and chopped
1 vegetable stock cube
2.5ml/½ tsp ground allspice
2 carrots
115g/4oz white cabbage
175g/6oz okra
½ red pepper, seeded
150ml/¼ pint/⅔ cup vegetable stock
salt

1 Heat the oil in a large saucepan and fry the onion and garlic over a moderate heat for 5 minutes, stirring frequently. Add the tomatoes and peanut butter and stir well.

2 Stir in the water, thyme, chilli, stock cube, allspice and a little salt. Bring to the boil and then simmer gently, uncovered for about 35 minutes.

3 Cut the carrots into sticks, slice the cabbage, top and tail the okra and seed and slice the red pepper.

4 Place the vegetables in a saucepan with the stock, bring to the boil and cook until tender but still with a little "bite".

5 Drain the vegetables and place in a warmed serving dish. Pour the sauce over the top and serve.

Marinated Vegetables on Skewers

These kebabs are a delightful main dish for vegetarians, or serve them as a vegetable side dish.

INGREDIENTS

Serves 4

115g/4oz pumpkin
1 red onion
1 small courgette
1 ripe plantain
1 aubergine
1/2 red pepper, seeded
1/2 green pepper, seeded
12 button mushrooms
60ml/4 tbsp lemon juice
60ml/4 tbsp olive or sunflower oil
45–60ml/3–4 tbsp soy sauce
150ml/1/4 pint/2/3 cup tomato juice
1 green chilli, seeded and chopped
1/2 onion, grated
3 garlic cloves, crushed
7.5ml/1 1/2 tsp dried tarragon, crushed
4ml/3/4 tsp dried basil
4ml/3/4 tsp dried thyme
4ml/3/4 tsp ground cinnamon
25g/1oz/2 tbsp butter or margarine
300ml/1/2 pint/1 1/4 cups vegetable stock
freshly ground black pepper
fresh parsley sprigs, to garnish

1 Peel and cube the pumpkin, place in a small bowl and cover with boiling water. Blanch for 2–3 minutes, then drain and refresh under cold water.

2 Cut the onion into wedges, slice the courgette and plantain and cut the aubergine and red and green peppers into chunks. Trim the mushrooms. Place the vegetables, including the pumpkin in a large bowl.

3 Mix together the lemon juice, oil, soy sauce, tomato juice, chilli, grated onion, garlic, herbs, cinnamon and black pepper and pour over the vegetables. Toss together and then set aside in a cool place to marinate for a few hours.

4 Thread the vegetables on to eight skewers, using a variety of vegetables on each to make a colourful display. Preheat the grill.

5 Grill the vegetables under a low heat, for about 15 minutes, turning frequently, until golden brown, basting with the marinade to keep the vegetables moist.

6 Place the remaining marinade, butter or margarine and stock in a pan and simmer for 10 minutes to cook the onion and reduce the sauce.

7 Pour the sauce into a serving jug and arrange the vegetable skewers on a plate. Garnish with parsley and serve with a rice dish or salad.

COOK'S TIP

You can use any vegetable that you prefer. Just first parboil any that may require longer cooking.

Black-eyed Bean Stew with Spicy Pumpkin

INGREDIENTS

Serves 3–4

225g/8oz/1¼ cups black-eyed beans,
  soaked for 4 hours or overnight
1 onion, chopped
1 green or red pepper, seeded and
  chopped
2 garlic cloves, chopped
1 vegetable stock cube
1 thyme sprig or 5ml/1 tsp dried thyme
5ml/1 tsp paprika
2.5ml/½ tsp mixed spice
2 carrots, sliced
15–30ml/1–2 tbsp palm oil
salt and hot pepper sauce

For the spicy pumpkin

675g/1½ lb pumpkin
1 onion
25g/1oz/2 tbsp butter or margarine
2 garlic cloves, crushed
3 tomatoes, peeled and chopped
2.5ml/½ tsp ground cinnamon
10ml/2 tsp curry powder
pinch of grated nutmeg
300ml/½ pint/⅔ cup water
salt, hot pepper sauce and freshly
  ground black pepper

1 Drain the beans, place in a pan and cover generously with water. Bring the beans to the boil.

2 Add the onion, green or red pepper, garlic, stock cube, herbs and spices. Simmer for 45 minutes or until the beans are just tender. Season to taste with the salt and a little hot pepper sauce.

3 Add the carrots and palm oil and continue cooking for about 10–12 minutes until the carrots are cooked, adding a little more water if necessary. Remove from the heat and set aside.

4 To make the spicy pumpkin, cut the pumpkin into cubes and finely chop the onion.

5 Melt the butter or margarine in a frying pan or saucepan, and add the pumpkin, onion, garlic, tomatoes, spices and water. Stir well to combine and simmer until the pumpkin is soft. Season with salt, hot pepper sauce and black pepper, to taste. Serve with the black-eyed beans.

Chick-peas, Sweet Potato and Garden Egg

Spicy and delicious – especially when served with Bulgur and Pine Nut Pilaff.

INGREDIENTS

Serves 3–4

45ml/3 tbsp olive oil
1 red onion, chopped
3 garlic cloves, crushed
115g/4oz sweet potatoes, peeled and diced
3 garden eggs or 1 large aubergine, diced
425g/15oz can chick-peas, drained
5ml/1 tsp dried tarragon
2.5ml/½ tsp dried thyme
5ml/1 tsp ground cumin
5ml/1 tsp ground turmeric
2.5ml/½ tsp ground allspice
5 canned plum tomatoes, chopped with 4 tbsp reserved juice
6 dried apricots
600ml/1 pint/2½ cups well-flavoured vegetable stock
1 green chilli, seeded and finely chopped
30ml/2 tbsp chopped fresh coriander
salt and freshly ground black pepper

1 Heat the olive oil in a large saucepan over a moderate heat. Add the onion, garlic and sweet potatoes and cook for about 5 minutes until the onion is slightly softened.

2 Stir in the garden eggs or aubergine, then add the chick-peas and the herbs and spices. Stir well to mix and cook over a gentle heat for a few minutes.

3 Add the tomatoes and their juice, the apricots, stock, chilli and seasoning. Stir well, bring slowly to the boil and cook for about 15 minutes.

4 When the sweet potatoes are tender, add the coriander, stir and adjust the seasoning if necessary.

COOK'S TIP

Garden egg is a small variety of aubergine used widely in West Africa. It is round and white, which may explain its other name – eggplant. You can peel the aubergine for this dish, if preferred, although it's not necessary. Either white or orange sweet potatoes can be used and you can add less chick-peas, if you wish.

SIDE DISHES

Although some classic vegetable dishes, like sweet potatoes and plantains are served by themselves, most African side dishes are a combination of vegetables, herbs and spices. A staple food like fufu or ground rice is always served with a meal but other side dishes can be served as well. Fu fu is a traditional African dish and can be made using various flours or root vegetables depending on the local crop. I've used yam and plantains in my Fufu recipe, which give it a pleasant mild flavour that goes well with the meat and poultry dishes. Breads, such as Mandazi or Coconut Chapatis are popular in many parts of the African continent, eaten either with the meal or as snacks during the day.

Bulgur and Pine Nut Pilaff

Pilaff is a popular staple in the Middle East. Here is a North African version.

INGREDIENTS

Serves 4

30ml/2 tbsp olive oil
1 onion, chopped
1 garlic clove, crushed
5ml/1 tsp ground saffron or turmeric
2.5ml/½ tsp ground cinnamon
1 green chilli, seeded and chopped
600ml/1 pint/2½ cups vegetable stock
150ml/¼ pint/⅔ cups white wine
225g/8oz/1⅓ cups bulgur wheat
15g/½ oz/1 tbsp butter or margarine
30–45ml/2–3 tbsp pine nuts
30ml/2 tbsp chopped fresh parsley

1 Heat the oil in a large saucepan and fry the onion until soft. Add the garlic, saffron or turmeric, ground cinnamon, and chopped chilli, and fry for a few seconds more.

2 Add the stock and wine, bring to the boil, then simmer for 8 minutes.

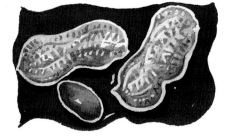

3 Rinse the bulgur wheat under cold water, drain and add to the stock. Cover and simmer gently for about 15 minutes until the stock is absorbed.

4 Melt the butter in a small pan, add the pine nuts and fry for a few minutes until golden. Add to the bulgur wheat with the chopped parsley and stir with a fork to mix.

5 Spoon into a warmed serving dish and serve with Chick-peas, Sweet Potato and Garden Egg or other vegetable or meat stew.

> — COOK'S TIP —
>
> You can leave out the wine, if you prefer and replace with water or stock. It's not essential, but it adds extra flavour.

Joloff Rice

INGREDIENTS

Serves 4

30ml/2 tbsp vegetable oil
1 large onion, chopped
2 garlic cloves, crushed
30ml/2 tbsp tomato purée
350g/12oz/1½ cups long grain rice
1 green chilli, seeded and chopped
600ml/1 pint/2½ cups vegetable or
  chicken stock

1 Heat the oil in a saucepan and fry the onion and garlic for 4–5 minutes until soft. Add the tomato purée and fry over a moderate heat for about 3 minutes, stirring all the time.

2 Rinse the rice in cold water, drain well and add to the pan with the chilli and a pinch of salt. Cook for 2–3 minutes, stirring all the time to prevent the rice sticking to the base of the pan.

3 Add the stock, bring to the boil, then cover and simmer over a low heat for about 15 minutes.

4 When the liquid is nearly absorbed, cover the rice with a piece of foil, cover the pan and steam, over a low heat, until the rice is cooked.

Gari Foto

INGREDIENTS

Serves 4

25g/1oz butter or margarine
1 onion, chopped
3 tomatoes, peeled and chopped
15ml/1 tbsp tomato purée
175g/6oz carrots, chopped
115g/4oz/²/₃ cup sweetcorn
175g/6oz red peppers, seeded and
  chopped
300ml/¹/₂ pint/1¹/₄ cup vegetable stock
  or water
1 green chilli, seeded and chopped
115g/4oz gari

2 Add the tomato purée and carrots and fry for a few minutes, then stir in the sweetcorn, red peppers, stock or water and chilli. Bring to the boil, then cover and simmer for 5 minutes.

3 Slowly mix the gari into the sauce, stirring constantly, until it is well mixed with the vegetables. Cover the saucepan and cook over a low heat for 5–8 minutes. Put into a serving dish and serve hot.

1 Melt the butter or margarine in a non-stick saucepan and fry the onion and tomatoes until pulpy, stirring frequently.

Ground Rice

Ground rice is served with soups and stews in West Africa.

INGREDIENTS

Serves 4

300ml/¹/₂ pint/1¹/₄ cups milk
300ml/¹/₂ pint/1¹/₄ cups water
25g/1oz/2 tbsp butter or margarine
2.5ml/¹/₂ tsp salt
15ml/1 tbsp chopped fresh parsley
275g/10oz/1¹/₂ cups ground rice

2 Add the ground rice, stirring vigorously with a wooden spoon to prevent the rice becoming lumpy.

3 Cover the pan and cook over a low heat for about 15 minutes, beating the mixture regularly every two minutes to prevent lumps forming.

4 To test if the rice is cooked, rub a pinch of the mixture between your fingers; if it feels smooth and fairly dry, it is ready. Serve hot.

1 Place the milk, water and butter or margarine in a saucepan, bring to the boil and add the salt and parsley.

COOK'S TIP

Ground rice is creamy white and when cooked has a slightly grainy texture. Although often used here in sweet dishes, it is a tasty grain to serve with savoury dishes too. The addition of milk makes it creamier, but it can be omitted if preferred.

Efua's Ghanaian Salad

INGREDIENTS

Serves 4

115g/4oz cooked, peeled prawns
1 garlic clove, crushed
7.5ml/½ tbsp vegetable oil
2 eggs
1 yellow plantain, halved
4 lettuce leaves
2 tomatoes
1 red pepper
1 avocado
juice of 1 lemon
1 carrot
200g/7oz can tuna or sardines
1 green chilli, finely chopped
30ml/2 tbsp chopped spring onion
salt and freshly ground black pepper

1 Put the prawns in a small bowl, add the garlic and a little seasoning.

2 Heat the oil in a small saucepan, add the prawns and cook over a low heat for a few minutes. Transfer to a plate to cool.

3 Hard-boil the eggs, place in cold water to cool, then shell and cut into slices.

4 Boil the plantain in a pan of water for 15 minutes, cool, then peel and slice thickly.

5 Shred the lettuce and arrange on a large serving plate. Slice the tomatoes and red pepper and peel and slice the avocado, sprinkling it with a little lemon juice. Arrange vegetables on the plate. Cut the carrot into matchstick-size pieces and arrange over the lettuce with the other vegetables.

6 Add the plantain, eggs, prawns and tuna fish or sardines. Sprinkle with the remaining lemon juice, scatter the chilli and spring onion on top and season with salt and pepper to taste. Serve as a lunch-time salad or as a delicious side dish.

COOK'S TIP

To make a complete meal, serve this salad with a meat or fish dish. Vary the ingredients, use any canned fish and a mixture of interesting lettuce leaves.

Plantain and Green Banana Salad

The plantains and bananas may be cooked in their skins to retain their soft texture. They will then absorb all the flavour of the dressing.

INGREDIENTS

Serves 4

2 firm yellow plantains
3 green bananas
1 garlic clove, crushed
1 red onion
15–30ml/1–2 tbsp chopped fresh
    coriander
45ml/3 tbsp sunflower oil
22.5ml/1½ tbsp malt vinegar
salt and coarse grain black pepper

1 Slit the plantains and bananas lengthways along their natural ridges, then cut in half and place in a large saucepan.

2 Cover the plantains and bananas with water, add a little salt and bring to the boil. Boil gently for 20 minutes until tender, then remove from the water. When they are cool enough to handle, peel and cut into medium-size slices.

3 Put the plantain and banana slices into a bowl and add the garlic, turning to mix.

4 Halve the onion and slice thinly. Add to the bowl with the coriander, oil, vinegar and seasoning. Toss together to mix, then serve as an accompaniment to a main dish.

Cameroon Coconut Rice

A special treat from Buea. Use thin coconut milk, which is rich enough and won't dominate the other ingredients.

INGREDIENTS

Serves 4

30ml/2 tbsp vegetable oil
1 onion, chopped
30ml/2 tbsp tomato purée
600ml/1 pint/2½ cups coconut milk
2 carrots, chopped
1 yellow pepper, seeded and chopped
5ml/1 tsp dried thyme
2.5ml/½ tsp mixed spice
1 fresh green chilli, seeded and chopped
350g/12oz/1½ cups long grain rice
salt

1 Heat the oil in a large saucepan and fry the onion for 2 minutes. Add the tomato purée and cook over a moderate heat for 5–6 minutes, stirring all the time. Add the coconut milk, stir well and bring to the boil.

2 Roughly chop the carrots and chop the pepper, discarding the seeds.

3 Stir the carrots, pepper, thyme, mixed spice, chilli and rice into the onion mixture, season with salt and bring to the boil. Cover and cook over a low heat until the rice has absorbed most of the liquid. Cover the rice with foil, secure with the lid and steam very gently until the rice is done. Serve hot.

Chick-pea and Okra Fry

Other vegetables can be added to this stir-fry to make a pleasing side dish. Mushrooms, cooked potatoes, courgettes or french beans would all be suitable additions.

INGREDIENTS

Serves 4

450g/1lb okra
15ml/1 tbsp vegetable oil
15ml/1 tbsp mustard oil
15g/½oz/1 tbsp butter or margarine
1 onion, finely chopped
1 garlic clove, crushed
2 tomatoes, finely chopped
1 green chilli, seeded and finely chopped
2 slices fresh root ginger
5ml/1 tsp ground cumin
15ml/1 tbsp chopped fresh coriander
425g/15oz can chick-peas, drained
salt and freshly ground black pepper

1 Wash and dry the okra, remove the tops and tails and chop roughly.

2 Heat the vegetable and mustard oils and the butter or margarine in a large frying pan.

3 Fry the onion and garlic for 5 minutes until the onion is slightly softened. Add the chopped tomatoes, chilli and ginger and stir well, then add the okra, cumin and coriander. Simmer for 5 minutes, stirring frequently then stir in the chick-peas and a little seasoning.

4 Cook gently for a few minutes for the chick-peas to heat through, then spoon into a serving bowl and serve at once.

Tanzanian Vegetable Rice

Serve this tasty rice with baked chicken, or a fish dish and a delicious fresh relish – Kachumbali. The vegetables are added towards the end of cooking, so that they retain their crisp texture.

INGREDIENTS

Serves 4
350g/12oz/1½ cups basmati rice
45ml/3 tbsp vegetable oil
1 onion, chopped
2 garlic cloves, crushed
750ml/1¼ pints/3 cups vegetable stock
  or water
115g/4oz/⅔ cup sweetcorn
½ red or green pepper, chopped
1 large carrot, grated

1 Wash the rice in a sieve under cold water, then leave to drain for about 15 minutes.

2 Heat the oil in a large saucepan and fry the onion for a few minutes over a moderate heat until just soft.

3 Add the rice and stir-fry for about 10 minutes, taking care to keep stirring all the time so that the rice doesn't stick to the pan.

4 Add the garlic and the stock or water and stir well. Bring to the boil and cook over a high heat for 5 minutes, then reduce the heat, cover and cook the rice for 20 minutes.

5 Scatter the corn over the rice, then spread the pepper on top and lastly sprinkle over the grated carrot.

6 Cover tightly and steam over a low heat until the rice is cooked, then mix together with a fork and serve immediately.

COOK'S TIP

If the rice begins to dry out, add a little more stock or water, but make sure not to overcook the rice – it should be tender but not soft.

Kenyan Mung Bean Stew

The Kenyan name for this simple and tasty stew is *Dengu*.

INGREDIENTS

Serves 4

225g/8oz/1¼ cups mung beans soaked overnight
25g/1oz/2 tbsp ghee or butter
2 garlic cloves, crushed
1 red onion, chopped
30ml/2 tbsp tomato purée
½ green pepper, seeded and cut into small cubes
½ red pepper, seeded and cut into small cubes
1 green chilli, seeded and finely chopped
300ml/½ pint/1¼ cups water

1 Put the mung beans in a large saucepan, cover with water and boil until the beans are soft and the water has evaporated. Remove from the heat and mash roughly with a fork or potato masher until smooth.

2 Heat the ghee or butter in a separate saucepan, add the garlic and onion and fry for 4–5 minutes until golden brown, then add the tomato purée and cook for a further 2–3 minutes, stirring all the time.

3 Stir in the mashed beans, then the green and red peppers and chilli.

4 Add the water, stirring well to mix all the ingredients together.

5 Pour back into a clean saucepan and simmer for about 10 minutes, then spoon into a serving dish and serve at once.

COOK'S TIP

If you prefer a more traditional, smoother texture to your stew, cook the mung beans until they are very soft, then mash them thoroughly until smooth.

Coconut Chapatis

INGREDIENTS

Makes 9–10

450g/1lb/4 cups plain flour
2.5ml/¹⁄₂ tsp salt
300ml/¹⁄₂ pint/1¹⁄₄ cups coconut milk
vegetable oil, for shallow frying

1 Place the flour and salt in a large bowl and gradually stir in the coconut milk to make a soft dough. Bring together with your hand.

2 Turn the dough out on to a floured work surface and knead with your hands to form a firm but pliable dough, adding more flour if the dough is on the sticky side.

3 Break the dough into nine equal-size balls, and roll out each ball on a lightly floured surface to a 22cm/8¹⁄₂ in round.

4 Brush the rounds with oil, roll up and twist into a ring, tucking the ends into the middle. Place on a floured board and set aside for 15 minutes.

5 Roll out each of the dough rings to a 5cm/2in round. Brush a heavy frying pan with oil and cook the chapatis for 3–4 minutes on each side until golden brown. Serve hot as an accompaniment.

Mandazi

Serve these East African breads as a snack or as an accompaniment to a meal.

INGREDIENTS

Makes about 15

4 or 5 cardamom pods
450g/1lb/4 cups self-raising flour
45ml/3 tbsp caster sugar
5ml/1 tsp baking powder
1 egg, beaten
30ml/2 tbsp vegetable oil, plus oil for deep frying
225ml/7fl oz/⁷⁄₈ cup milk or water

1 Crush each cardamom pod, shake out the seeds and grind the seeds in a small mortar and pestle, then place in a large bowl with the flour, sugar and baking powder. Stir well to mix.

2 Put the egg and oil in a small bowl and beat together, then add to the flour mixture. Mix with your fingers, gradually adding the milk or water to make a dough.

3 Lightly knead the dough until smooth and not sticky when a finger is pushed into it, adding more flour if necessary. Leave in a warm place for 15 minutes, then roll out the dough on a floured surface to about a 1cm/¹⁄₂in thickness and cut into 6cm/2¹⁄₂in rounds.

4 Heat the oil in a heavy saucepan or deep-fat fryer and fry the mandazis for 4–5 minutes, until golden brown, turning frequently in the oil.

Yam Chips

INGREDIENTS

Serves 4
450g/1lb white yam
good pinch of chilli powder or cayenne
   pepper
salt and freshly ground black pepper
oil, for deep frying

1 Peel the yam and cut into slices, then into chips. Place the yam chips in a saucepan and cover with cold salted water.

2 Bring the water to the boil, cook for 5 minutes, then drain the chips in a colander or on kitchen paper for 5 minutes. Sprinkle with chilli powder or cayenne pepper.

COOK'S TIP

Only half-fill the pan with oil, as it will bubble up when the yam chips are added.

3 Heat the oil in a heavy saucepan or deep-fat fryer until hot, then fry the yam chips for about 6–8 minutes, until cooked through, golden brown and crisp.

4 Drain well, then tip into a dish lined with kitchen paper. Sprinkle with salt and serve immediately.

Yam and Plantain Fu Fu

INGREDIENTS

Serves 4
450g/1lb white yam
2 green plantains
15g/½ oz/1 tbsp butter or margarine
salt and black or white pepper

1 Peel, wash and slice the yam and place in a saucepan, then cover with cold salted water.

2 Cut the green plantains in half, slit along the natural ridges in three places and remove the skins. Put the plantains in the saucepan with the yam, bring to the boil and cook for about 25 minutes until the vegetables are tender.

3 Drain the vegetables and place in a blender or food processor. Add the butter or margarine, season well with salt and pepper, and process until smooth and lump free.

4 Turn the fu fu into a bowl, then take small handfuls and shape into balls. Serve with casseroles and stews.

COOK'S TIP

This dish is especially good served as an accompaniment to Groundnut Soup or Fish and Okra Soup as a main meal.

Ethiopian Collard Greens

Also known as *Abesha Gomen*, this dish is simple and delicious. Use spring greens in place of the collard greens if you are unable to get the real thing.

INGREDIENTS

Serves 4

450g/1lb collard greens
60ml/4 tbsp olive oil
2 small red onions, finely chopped
1 garlic clove, crushed
2.5ml/½ tsp grated fresh root ginger
2 green chillies, seeded and sliced
150ml/¼ pint/⅔ cup vegetable stock or
    water
1 red pepper, seeded and sliced
salt and freshly ground black pepper

1 Wash the collard greens, then strip the leaves from the stalks and steam the leaves over a pan of boiling water for about 5 minutes until slightly wilted. Set aside on a plate to cool, then place in a sieve or colander and press out the excess water.

2 Using a large sharp knife, slice the collard greens very thinly.

3 Heat the oil in a saucepan and fry the onions until browned. Add the garlic and ginger and stir-fry with the onions for a few minutes, then add the chillies and a little of the stock or water and cook for 2 minutes.

4 Add the greens, red pepper and the remaining stock or water. Season with salt and pepper, mix well, then cover and cook over a low heat for about 15 minutes.

--- COOK'S TIP ---

Traditionally this dish is cooked with more liquid and for longer. The cooking time has been reduced from 45 minutes to 15 minutes. However, if you fancy a more authentic taste, cook for longer and increase the amount of liquid. Green Cabbage is a good substitute for collard greens.

Green Lentil Salad

Azifa is the African name for this piquant, colourful salad.

INGREDIENTS

Serves 4

225g/8oz/1 cup green lentils, soaked
    overnight
2 tomatoes, peeled and chopped
1 red onion, finely chopped
1 green chilli, seeded and chopped
60ml/4 tbsp lemon juice
75ml/5 tbsp olive oil
2.5ml/½ tsp prepared mustard
salt and freshly ground black pepper

1 Place the lentils in a saucepan, cover with water and bring to the boil. Simmer for 45 minutes until soft, drain, then turn into a bowl and mash lightly with a potato masher or fork.

2 Add the tomatoes, onion, chilli, lemon juice, olive oil, mustard and seasoning. Mix well, adjust seasoning if necessary, then chill before serving as an accompaniment to a meat or fish dish.

Kachumbali

Kachumbali is a peppery relish from Tanzania, where it is served with grilled meat or fish dishes, together with rice – this salad uses the same combination of vegetables and flavours.

INGREDIENTS

Serves 4–6
2 red onions
4 tomatoes
1 green chilli
½ cucumber
1 carrot
juice of 1 lemon
salt and freshly ground black pepper

1 Slice the onions and tomatoes very thinly and place in a bowl.

2 Slice the chilli lengthways, discard the seeds, then chop very finely. Peel and slice the cucumber and carrot and add to the onions and tomatoes.

3 Squeeze the lemon juice over the salad. Season with salt and freshly ground black pepper and toss together to mix. Serve as an accompaniment, salad or relish.

--- COOK'S TIP ---

Traditional *Kachumbali* is made by very finely chopping the onions, tomatoes, cucumber and carrot. This produces a very moist, sauce-like mixture, which is good served inside chapatis, and eaten as a snack.

Coconut Relish

This simple but delicious relish is widely made in Tanzania. Only the white part of the coconut flesh is used – either shred it fairly coarsely, or grate it finely for a moister result.

INGREDIENTS

Makes about 50g/2oz
50g/2oz fresh or desiccated coconut
10ml/2 tsp lemon juice
1.5ml/¼ tsp salt
10ml/2 tsp water
1.5ml/¼ tsp finely chopped red chilli

1 Grate the coconut and place in a mixing bowl. If using desiccated coconut, add just enough water to moisten it.

2 Add the lemon juice, salt, water and chilli. Stir thoroughly and serve as a relish with meats or as an accompaniment to a main dish.

DESSERTS

*In a continent like Africa, where fruit is cheap,
plentiful and completely fresh, it's not surprising
that it's eaten at any time of the day, whenever
people fancy. Market stalls are full of luscious fruit
– pineapples, mangoes and spicy smelling guavas
– and it's not unusual for fruit trees to grow in
your garden, there just for the picking. Fruit is
also served at the end of the meal but desserts are
not a strong feature of African cuisine and apart
from Banana Mandazi, most of the recipes in this
section are my own creations. My resistance level
to coconut is low, hence its presence in many of the
recipes. If you're not as partial to it as me,
use it a little more moderately!*

Fresh Pineapple with Coconut

This refreshing dessert can also be made with vacuum-packed pineapple. This makes a good substitute, but fresh is best.

INGREDIENTS

Serves 4
1 fresh pineapple, peeled
slivers of fresh coconut
300ml/½ pint/1¼ cups pineapple juice
60ml/4 tbsp coconut liqueur
2.5cm/1in piece stem ginger, plus
    45ml/3 tbsp of the syrup

1 Peel and slice the pineapple, arrange in a serving dish and scatter the coconut slivers on top.

2 Place the pineapple juice and coconut liqueur in a saucepan and heat gently.

3 Thinly slice the stem ginger and add to the pan along with the ginger syrup. Bring just to the boil and then simmer gently until the liquid is slightly reduced and the sauce is fairly thick.

4 Pour the sauce over the pineapple and coconut, leave to cool, then chill before serving.

COOK'S TIP

If fresh coconut is not available, then use desiccated coconut instead.

Spiced Nutty Bananas

Cinnamon and nutmeg are spices which perfectly complement bananas in this delectable dessert.

INGREDIENTS

Serves 3

6 ripe, but firm, bananas
30ml/2 tbsp chopped unsalted cashew nuts
30ml/2 tbsp chopped unsalted peanuts
30ml/2 tbsp desiccated coconut
7.5–15ml/¹⁄₂–1 tbsp demerara sugar
5ml/1 tsp ground cinnamon
2.5ml/¹⁄₂ tsp freshly grated nutmeg
150ml/¹⁄₄ pint/²⁄₃ cup orange juice
60ml/4 tbsp rum
15g/¹⁄₂ oz/1 tbsp butter or margarine
double cream, to serve

1 Preheat the oven to 200°C/400°F/ Gas 6. Slice the bananas and place in a greased, shallow ovenproof dish.

2 Mix together the cashew nuts, peanuts, coconut, sugar, cinnamon and nutmeg in a small bowl.

3 Pour the orange juice and rum over the bananas, then sprinkle with the nut and sugar mixture.

4 Dot the top with butter or margarine, then bake in the oven for 15–20 minutes or until the bananas are golden and the sauce is bubbly. Serve with double cream.

COOK'S TIP

Freshly grated nutmeg makes all the difference to this dish. More rum can be added if preferred. Chopped mixed nuts can be used instead of peanuts.

Banana and Melon in Orange Vanilla Sauce

Most large supermarkets and health food shops sell vanilla pods. If vanilla pods are hard to find, use a few drops of natural vanilla essence instead.

INGREDIENTS

Serves 4

300ml/½ pint/1¼ cups orange juice
1 vanilla pod or a few drops vanilla essence
5ml/1 tsp grated orange rind
15ml/1 tbsp sugar
4 bananas
1 honeydew melon
30ml/2 tbsp lemon juice

1 Place the orange juice in a small saucepan with the vanilla pod, orange rind and sugar and gently bring to the boil.

2 Reduce the heat and simmer gently for 15 minutes or until the sauce is syrupy. Remove from the heat and leave to cool. If using vanilla essence, stir into the sauce when cool.

3 Roughly chop the bananas and melon, place in a large serving bowl and toss with the lemon juice.

4 Pour the cooled sauce over the fruit and chill before serving.

Banana Mandazi

INGREDIENTS

Serves 4

1 egg
2 ripe bananas, roughly chopped
150ml/¼ pint/⅔ cup milk
2.5ml/½ tsp vanilla essence
225g/8oz/2 cups self-raising flour
5ml/1 tsp baking powder
45ml/3 tbsp sugar
vegetable oil, for deep frying

1 Place the egg, bananas, milk, vanilla essence, flour, baking powder and sugar in a blender or food processor.

2 Process to make a smooth batter. It should have a creamy dropping consistency. If it is too thick, add a little extra milk. Set aside for 10 minutes.

3 Heat the oil in a heavy saucepan or deep-fat fryer. When hot, carefully place spoonfuls of the mixture in the oil and fry for 3–4 minutes until golden. Remove with a slotted spoon and drain on kitchen paper. Keep warm while cooking the remaining mandazis, then serve at once.

Tropical Fruit Pancakes

INGREDIENTS

Serves 4

115g/4oz/1 cup self-raising flour
pinch of grated nutmeg
15ml/1 tbsp caster sugar
1 egg
300ml/¹⁄₂ pint/1¹⁄₄ cups milk
15ml/1 tbsp melted butter or
  margarine, plus extra for frying
15ml/1 tbsp fine desiccated coconut
  (optional)
fresh cream, to serve

For the filling

225g/8oz ripe, firm mango
2 bananas
2 kiwi fruit
1 large orange
15ml/1 tbsp lemon juice
30ml/2 tbsp orange juice
15ml/1 tbsp honey
30–45ml/2–3 tbsp orange liqueur
  (optional)

1 Sift the flour, nutmeg and caster sugar into a large bowl. In a separate bowl, beat the egg lightly, then beat in most of the milk. Add to the flour mixture and beat with a wooden spoon to make a thick, smooth batter.

2 Add the remaining milk, butter and coconut, if using, and continue beating until the batter is smooth and of a fairly thin, dropping consistency.

3 Melt a little butter or margarine in a large non-stick frying pan. Swirl to cover the pan, then pour in a little batter to cover the base of the pan. Fry until golden brown, then toss or turn with a spatula. Repeat with the remaining mixture to make about eight pancakes.

4 Dice the mango, roughly chop the bananas and slice the kiwi fruit. Cut away the peel and pith from the orange and cut into segments.

5 Place the fruit in a bowl. Mix the lemon and orange juices, honey and orange liqueur, if using, then pour over the fruit.

6 Spoon a little fruit down the centre of a pancake and fold over each side. Repeat with the remaining pancakes, then serve with fresh cream.

Paw Paw and Mango with Mango Cream

INGREDIENTS

Serves 4

2 large ripe mangoes
300ml/½ pint/1¼ cups extra thick
   double cream
8 dried apricots, halved
150ml/¼ pint/⅔ cup orange juice or
   water
1 ripe paw paw

1 Take one thick slice from one of
the mangoes and, while still on the
skin, slash the flesh with a sharp knife
in a criss-cross pattern to make cubes.

2 Turn the piece of mango inside-
out and cut away the cubed flesh
from the skin. Place in a bowl, mash
with a fork to a pulp, then add the
cream and mix together well. Spoon
into a freezer tub and freeze for about
1–1½ hours until half frozen.

3 Meanwhile, put the apricots and
orange juice or water in a small
saucepan. Bring to the boil, then
simmer gently until the apricots are
soft, adding a little more juice or water
if necessary, so that the apricots remain
moist. Remove from the heat and set
aside to cool.

4 Chop or dice the remaining
mangoes as above and place in a
bowl. Cut the paw paw in half, remove
the seeds and peel. Dice the flesh and
add to the mango.

5 Pour the apricot sauce over the
fruit and gently toss together so the
fruit is well coated.

6 Stir the semi-frozen mango cream
a few times until spoonable but
not soft. Serve the fruit topped with
the mango cream.

─── COOK'S TIP ───

Mangoes vary tremendously in size. If you
can only find small ones, buy three instead
of two to use in this dessert.

Index

Akkras, 22
Aubergines: beef in aubergine
    sauce, 32
    chick-peas, sweet potato and
      garden egg, 67
    fish with crab meat and
      aubergine, 50
Avocado and smoked fish salad, 24

Bananas: banana and melon in
    orange vanilla sauce, 92
    banana mandazi, 92
    plantain and green banana
      salad, 75
    spiced nutty bananas, 91
    tropical fruit pancakes, 94
Beef: beef in aubergine sauce, 32
    Cameroon suya, 22
    kofta curry, 29
    Nigerian meat stew, 28
    spicy kebabs, 20
Black-eyed beans: akkras, 22
    black-eyed bean stew with
      spicy pumpkin, 66
    lamb, bean and pumpkin
      soup, 12
    mutton with black-eyed beans
      and pumpkin, 33
Bulgur wheat: bulgur and pine nut
    pilaff, 70

Cameroon suya, 22
Cashew nuts: spiced nutty
    bananas, 91
Chick-peas: chick-pea and okra
    fry, 76
    chick-peas, sweet potato and
      garden egg, 67
Chicken: chicken with lentils, 41
    chicken, tomato and
      christophene soup, 16
    East African roast chicken, 38
    joloff chicken and rice, 40
    Nigerian meat stew, 28
    palava chicken, 42
    yassa chicken, 38
Christophene: chicken, tomato
    and christophene soup, 16
Coconut: Cameroon coconut
    rice, 76
    coconut chapatis, 80
    coconut relish, 86
    fish and prawns with spinach
      and coconut, 48
    fresh pineapple with
      coconut, 90
    fried pomfret in coconut
      sauce, 54
    makande, 60
    vegetable soup with coconut, 17
Collard greens: Ethiopian collard
    greens, 84
Coriander: fish with lemon, red
    onions and coriander, 53
    lamb tagine with coriander and
      spices, 35
Curry: kofta curry, 29
    lamb and vegetable pilau, 30
    Tanzanian fish curry, 49

Donu's lobster piri piri, 56

Dried shrimps: Donu's lobster piri
    piri, 56
    joloff chicken and rice, 40
Duck with sherry and pumpkin, 43

East African roast chicken, 38
Efua's Ghanaian salad, 74
Egusi spinach and egg, 62

Fish: fish and okra soup, 13
    fish and prawns with spinach
      and coconut, 48
    fish with crab meat and
      aubergine, 50
    fish with lemon, red onions and
      coriander, 53
    Tanzanian fish curry, 49

Garden eggs: chick-peas, sweet
    potato and garden egg, 67
Gari: bean and gari loaf, 63
    gari foto, 72

Kachumbali salad, 86
Kebabs: spicy kebabs, 20
Kenyan mung bean stew, 79
Kidney beans: bean and gari loaf, 63
    makande, 60
Kiwi fruit: tropical fruit
    pancakes, 94
Kofta curry, 29

Lamb: kofta curry, 29
    lamb and vegetable pilau, 30
    lamb, bean and pumpkin
      soup, 12
    lamb tagine with coriander and
      spices, 35
    mutton with black-eyed beans
      and pumpkin, 33
    roast lamb with saffron and
      tomatoes, 36
    spiced fried lamb, 34
Lemon: fish with lemon, red
    onions and coriander, 53
    stuffed turkey fillets in lemon
      sauce, 44
Lentils: chicken with lentils, 41
    green lentil salad, 84
Lobster: Donu's lobster piri piri, 56

Makande, 60
Mandazi, 80
Mangoes: paw paw and mango
    with mango cream, 95
    tilapia in turmeric, mango and
      tomato sauce, 57
    tropical fruit pancakes, 94
Marinated vegetables on skewers, 65
Melon: banana and melon in
    orange vanilla sauce, 92
Mung beans: chicken with
    lentils, 41
    Kenyan mung bean stew, 79
Mutton with black-eyed beans and
    pumpkin, 33

Okra: chick-pea and okra fry, 76
    fish and okra soup, 13
    groundnut soup, 14
    vegetables in peanut sauce, 64

Onions: fish with lemon, red
    onions and coriander, 53
    kachumbali, 86
Oranges: banana and melon in
    orange vanilla sauce, 92
    tropical fruit pancakes, 94
Oxtail: Nigerian meat stew, 28

Palava chicken, 42
Pancakes: tropical fruit pancakes, 94
Paw paw and mango with mango
    cream, 95
Peanut butter: groundnut soup, 14
    palava chicken, 42
    Tanzanian fish curry, 49
    vegetables in peanut sauce, 64
Peanuts: spiced nutty bananas, 91
Pine nuts: bulgur and pine nut
    pilaff, 70
Pineapple: fresh pineapple with
    coconut, 90
Plantains: assiette of plantains, 21
    Efua's Ghanaian salad, 74
    plantain and corn soup, 14
    plantain and green banana
      salad, 75
    sese plantain and yam, 60
    tatale, 18
    yam and plantain fu fu, 82
Pomfret: fried pomfret in coconut
    sauce, 54
Prawns: Donu's lobster piri piri, 56
    Efua's Ghanaian salad, 74
    fish and prawns with spinach
      and coconut, 48
    king prawns in almond sauce, 54
    king prawns with spicy dip, 25
    stuffed turkey fillets in lemon
      sauce, 44
Pumpkin: black-eyed bean stew
    with spicy pumpkin, 66
    duck with sherry and
      pumpkin, 43
    lamb, bean and pumpkin
      soup, 12
    mutton with black-eyed beans
      and pumpkin, 33
    vegetable soup with coconut, 17

Red snapper: baked red snapper, 52
    Tanzanian fish curry, 49
Rice: Cameroon coconut rice, 76
    ground rice, 72
    joloff chicken and rice, 40
    joloff rice, 70
    Lamb and vegetable pilau, 30
    Tanzanian vegetable rice, 78
Roast lamb with saffron and
    tomatoes, 36

Salad: avocado and smoked fish
    salad, 24
    Efua's Ghanaian salad, 74
    green lentil salad, 84
    kachumbali salad, 86
    plantain and green banana
      salad, 75
Salmon: fish with crab meat and
    aubergine, 50
Sese plantain and yam, 60
Shrimps: Donu's lobster piri piri, 56

joloff chicken and rice, 40
Smoked haddock: chicken, tomato
    and christophene soup, 16
    fish and okra soup, 13
Smoked mackerel: avocado and
    smoked fish salad, 24
Soup: chicken, tomato and
    christophene soup, 16
    fish and okra soup, 13
    groundnut soup, 14
    lamb, bean and pumpkin
      soup, 12
    plantain and corn soup, 14
    vegetable soup with coconut, 17
Spiced fried lamb, 34
Spiced nutty bananas, 91
Spinach: egusi spinach and egg, 62
    fish and prawns with spinach
      and coconut, 48
    palava chicken, 42
Stews: black-eyed bean stew with
    spicy pumpkin, 66
    fried pomfret in coconut
      sauce, 54
    Kenyan mung bean stew, 79
    Nigerian meat stew, 28
Stuffed turkey fillets in lemon
    sauce, 44
Sweet potatoes: chick-peas, sweet
    potato and garden egg, 67
    stuffed turkey fillets in lemon
      sauce, 44
Sweetcorn: makande, 60
    plantain and corn soup, 14

Tanzanian fish curry, 49
Tanzanian vegetable rice, 78
Tatale, 18
Tilapia in turmeric, mango and
    tomato sauce, 57
Tomatoes:
    chicken, tomato and
      christophene soup, 16
    kachumbali, 86
    roast lamb with saffron and
      tomatoes, 36
    tilapia in turmeric, mango and
      tomato sauce, 57
    vegetables in peanut sauce, 64
Tropical fruit pancakes, 94
Turkey: stuffed turkey fillets in
    lemon sauce, 44

Vanilla: banana and melon in
    orange vanilla sauce, 92
Vegetables: gari foto, 72
    lamb and vegetable pilau, 30
    marinated vegetables on
      skewers, 65
    Tanzanian vegetable rice, 78
    vegetable soup with coconut, 17
    vegetables in peanut sauce, 64

Yams: groundnut soup, 14
    sese plantain and yam, 60
    yam balls, 18
    yam chips, 82
    yam and plantain fu fu, 82
Yassa chicken, 38